SENIOR SCENE

To Russ
all the best
as you near
your seniority

Ted Fuller

Also by Ted Fuller

San Diego Originals: Profiles of the
Movers and Shakers of
California's First Community
(Winner of a California Historical Society
Local History Award of Merit)

Seniors Acting Up: Humorous
New One-act Plays and
Skits for Older Adults
—Editor

Barney the Bus (A picture
book for children 3 to 7)

The MESA Way: A Success
Story of Nurturing Minorities
for Math/Science Careers
—Co-author

SENIOR
SCENE

BY
TED FULLER

PLEASANT HILL PRESS, PLEASANT HILL, CALIFORNIA

Published by:
Pleasant Hill Press
241 Greenwich Drive
Pleasant Hill, CA 94523

Selection of his columns appearing originally in the
Concord (California) Transcript, Martinez Record,
Pleasant Hill Record and the Walnut Creek Journal
December, 1995 – January, 1998

Fuller, Ted   1928-

LCNN number 98-15818 CIP

ISBN 0-9649776-1-2

First Printing May, 1998

Printed in the United States of America by:
Amazing Experiences Press
1908 Keswick Lane
Concord, CA 94518
(925) 691-5204
http://www.booksprinted.com

10   9   8   7   6   5   4   3   2   1

CONTENTS

ACKNOWLEDGMENTS

My wife, Betty Ann—often referred to in this opus as my perpetual sunbeam because of her sunny disposition and because a sunbeam can at times make you hot under the collar—encouraged and supported me and took me out to dinner when deadlines caused unruly stomach sensations.

After Ruth Stenson discovered she lacked the time to write a weekly newspaper column, she suggested my name and Concord (California) Transcript editor Dick Sparrer, unable at the time to conduct a thorough background search, hired me. He and Dolores Ciardelli, caught my goofs before my work appeared in print, and be assured those that crept back in this tome are of my own making. The newspaper's staff has been supportive and covered for me frequently.

Suggestions also came from my agent, Pat Edwards, but I went ahead with this project anyway.

Gentle and infrequent were the critiques from Alma Den, my writing group, mainly because at our age we meet much less frequently and then mostly to socialize. The Mt. Diablo Branch of the California Writers Club provided lots of helpful tips, especially from Ray Martell, and strokes as well

At the Central Contra Costa County Senior Coalition there exists a membership so open they let me serve three years as executive director and offered several times to raise my $1 annual salary, not realizing the treasury couldn't handle it. But they gave me good ideas and encouragement instead, as did members of the Pleasant Hill Commission on Aging, the staff members and volunteers at the Concord, Martinez, Pleasant Hill, San Ramon and Walnut Creek senior centers, the Contra Costa County Office on Aging, and many others to whom I am also indebted.

FOREWORD

It's an interesting time to grow old. Despite melatonin and DHEA, the inexorable march of time continues. Despite exciting research findings on the brain and memory, many of us can't recall what we ate for lunch yesterday. And despite the things we know for sure about nutrition and exercise, the majority of us are over-weight and under-active.

Nonetheless, record-breaking numbers of seniors are joining the ranks of the centenarians. The 85-plus group is the fastest growing segment of the population.

How to account for these seeming contradictions?

My theory is that our generation has learned—oftentimes the hard way—you can't take yourself too seriously. For example, we promulgated Kilroy in World War II; Murphy's Law followed close behind. We beamed when "Hut-sut Ralston" made the "Hit Parade."Our crowd endorsed the erudite sayings of a Paul Harvey, who declared, "In times like these, it is helpful to remember that there have always been times like these."

We learned from experience the truth of Alan Hinds' observation: "Man is planned obsolescence." (He made the observation soon after throwing his back out in Marion, Ohio.) We also learned how challenging it is to make something foolproof because fools are so clever.

This trait of not taking ourselves seriously will see us through the HMO debacle, the revamping of Social Security, the rescue of Medicare. It will stand us in good stead in the fuss about political campaign contributions, scandals and perfumed magazine ads.

And it is in this spirit that many of the following columns came into being. Fortunately, the others offer solutions to many of the major issues, thus providing you, the reader, with the best of several possible worlds.

TAKE ONE DAILY

Ted's HMO offers many benefits

You may have wondered why all those HMOs have been wooing and pursuing your business lately. I found the answer at a workshop the other day for a company I'll call Safe Spot Where Sky and Earth Appear to Meet.

It offers good benefits and no premiums. You can undergo an annual physical for $6. You receive 100 percent coverage for a hospital stay for an unlimited time.

(Hospital stays add up because the average cost per day is $1,500—an amount that starts doubling if you need aspirin or turn on a TV.)

The workshop leader noted that the federal government pays an HMO about $400 per month per Medicare member. And that's when the idea dawned for Ted's HMO.

Let's look at the potential. I sign up you and 499,999 other seniors. That's $200 million per month; a tidy $2.4 billion annually. Let's say $1 billion goes out for people who get sick or injured. My profit is limited by government order to 2.7 percent of the gross, which means there's $680 million a year for my salary and handling the paperwork.

What should I do with the rest? Easy. Plow it into bigger and better benefits. Here's what you'll receive from Ted's HMO:

- House calls. After all, physicians need exercise like the rest of us, and they'll get it with the GP Bicycle Brigade.

- 24-hour massage service. This will be available at home or at the friendly massage parlor in town. Parlor visitors may opt for the Witnessed Protection Program.

- Friendly listener plan. You've got a complaint about the HMO or your neighbor or Uncle Henry, just call us. We'll listen sympathetically to everything except the rationale for rap and details of your last sigmoidoscopy.

- Emergency hangnail service. Doctors and hospitals ignore this need. There also will be home pedicures, because no one should suffer the shame, especially in this age of "Bay Watch," of leaving the house with unsightly toenails.

- Wrinkle analysis. With the plethora of skin rejuvenators on the market now, help is needed to find the best compound for the varied ridges, grooves and ruts engraved on some of us. Ted's HMO offers a $57 monthly deductible for the creams, and, if you're not completely satisfied with the baby's bottom result, you'll receive free plastic surgery. You can choose, for example, the "National Velvet" Liz Taylor or a "Baby Face" Barbara Stanwyck job.

- Electronic fitness machines. As a member, you'll be loaned at no cost the latest equipment that tones muscles and reduces fat while you watch TV or doze. Electricity not included.

Ted's HMO. The possibilities are endless.

I've gone broke with several enterprises almost as promising as the one described above.

Questions of the "golden years"

While soaking up some afternoon rays at the senior center, waiting in line for a flu shot, a trio behind me began comparing maladies and remedies, the challenge of climbing stairs, the hassles of doctor's visits. Finally Marjorie observed, "It must have been a 25-year-old who called them the 'Golden Years.'"

Ours is a household divided when it comes to flu shots. My perpetual sunbeam never gets one. Me? I read about the horrible agonies of the latest strain, and I line up dutifully for the annual jab. The scorecard: In the past decade neither one of us has caught the bug.

Which brings to mind the story about Billy Burke, the actress. She was dining in a restaurant near the table where a man kept sneezing and blowing his nose.

"I can see you're very uncomfortable," she said. "So I'll tell you what to do for a cold: drink lots of orange juice and take lots of aspirin. When you go to bed, cover yourself with as many blankets as you can find. Sweat the cold out. Believe me, I know what I'm talking about. I am Billie Burke of Hollywood."

The man smiled and introduced himself in return: "Thank you. I am Dr. Mayo of the Mayo Clinic."

At the senior center, three volunteers—Betty, Edna and Inge—helped with the overflow crowd. I imagine the figures hold true at your center: 206 of the 2,300 members help run the place. They worked 27,100 hours during the year. That's the equivalent of nearly 14 full time staff members and $216,800 in salaries that taxpayers do not have to pay.

There's another group to applaud: nursing home aides. You read about them only when the rare goofball neglects or mistreats a patient. But the big majority of them bestow TLC under trying conditions for modest wages. That's the gist of the message from Carol Kehoe. She's an adult education teacher working primarily with Alzheimer's patients. She also heads a CARE Committee that annually awards the top nursing home aides and support staffers such as

the kitchen crew and maintenance workers. Their co-workers and
the patients vote on who deserves the recognition. After hearing
Kehoe praise them, you get the impression the awards should be
daily.

There's some kind of award that Alliance Capital deserves too.
That's the company whose TV commercials depict an older couple
so stupid about financial planning they must now apply for work at
the neighborhood fast food outlet. I wouldn't give them a Cleo (the
ad industry's coveted prize for TV commercials), but maybe a
Theo, which recognizes the validity of the company's warning as
well as the demeaning way it's presented.

On the other hand, Dave Thomas of Wendy's illustrates how a
senior executive can convey a message with panache. The TV commercial with Dave in shirt sleeves at the fashion show suggests he
doesn't take himself too seriously even while earnestly extolling
Wendy's latest sandwich.

Having just watched the World Serious, the question occurs:
Why don't senior centers hold a bash for these contests; at least the
day games? And while we're at it, a Super Bowl Sunday party?
Sporting events are more fun with a crowd hollering, moaning and
second-guessing. Skip the golf and fishing shows, however, unless
the insomniacs demand them.

One thing I admire about the senior centers I visit: They're willing to experiment with a new course, a speaker on an unusual topic
or an activity with a twist, providing a few people show an interest.
The centers subscribe to a slogan I read recently. It says,
"Experiments never fail."

That may stem from the Thomas Edison school of invention,
but, wherever, it tells me there's much we can gain from a different
hobby, a place visited for the first time and meeting someone new.

Risky? Sometimes. But staying mired in the same rut is the
biggest risk of all.

---

*The world had an opening for me, I thought when starting out,
and, sure enough, I ended up in the hole.*

Getting old—or just more quotable?

"Aging is a question of mind over matter," said Satchel Paige. "If you don't mind, it doesn't matter."

That's one of my favorite sayings about the aging process. Here are some more aphorisms, plus other tidbits, to help you get started on the weekend:

"We do not stop playing because we grow old; we grow old because we stop playing."

"The older the violin, the sweeter the music."—Spotted on a sofa pillow.

"No day is so bad that it can't be fixed with a nap."—Carrie Snow

"Do not feel sorry for yourself; that's the best way to lose all your friends."—Malcolm Boyd

"Time flies! I'm already as old as my parents were when they were my age."—Ashleigh Brilliant.

"It's sad for a woman to reach the age
Where men consider her charmless,
But it's worse for a man to attain the age
Where the women consider him harmless."—Anon.

"Nostalgia isn't what it used to be."

"Youth and experience are no match for experience and treachery."

"Don't let worry kill you—let the church help."—noted in a church newsletter.

"Ours is the late, last wisdom of the afternoon. We know that love, like light, grows dearer toward the dark."—Archibald MacLeish

"Never look in a magnifying mirror."—Norma Lent

"The past is a ghost, the future a dream, and all we ever have is now."—Bill Cosby.

"Age doesn't matter unless you're a cheese."—Billie Burke

"Contrary to popular notions, IQ does not decrease with age. An excellent way to nourish the intellect and maintain alertness is to stay involved. Stimulating the mind with fresh and challenging material helps keep it in shape."—Alvin F. Poussaint, M.D.

"After retirement, you discover one thing that beats that second cup of morning coffee—a nice snooze."—Ted Fuller

"You can't turn back the clock. But you can wind it up again."—Bonnie Prudden, physical fitness author

"The older I grow, the more I distrust the familiar doctrine that age brings wisdom."—H. L. Mencken

"I think all this talk about age is foolish. Every time I'm one year older, everyone else is too."—Gloria Swanson

"An old man gives good advice in order to console himself for no longer being in condition to set a bad example."—La Rochefoucauld

"To me old age is always 15 years older than I am."—Bernard Baruch

"It's not how old you are but how you are old."

"The four stages of man are infancy, childhood, adolescence and obsolescence."—*A Child's Garden of Misinformation* by Art Linkletter

"Growing old is like being increasingly penalized for a crime you haven't committed."—Anthony Powell

"I never offered an opinion till I was 60, and then it was one which had been in our family for a century."—Benjamin Disraeli

"The secret of staying young is to live honestly, eat slowly and lie about your age."—Lucille Ball

"Experience is a comb which nature gives to men when they are bald."—Eastern proverb

"How old would you be if you didn't know how old you was?"—Satchel Paige

"Do not go gentle into that good night, old age should burn and rave at close of day; rage, rage against the dying of the light."—Dylan Thomas

---

Older adults need at least three books of quotations close at hand. And it's not just Bartlett who feels that way.

Info that can help you plan ahead

With help from Griselda, a psychic who predicted the Macarena, I am pleased to present a Seniors Horoscope:

ARIES (March 21-April 20): Exert your leadership qualities (some critics call it "bossiness") at the senior center. You could end up as a bingo caller, bazaar coordinator or movie shhhsher. Because of the conjunction of Venus and Mars, you could influence the loosening of purse strings for, say, a new seniors' language comprehension program called Elderonics.

TAURUS (April 21-May 21): Allow a bit of leeway even when an old love forgets your birthday. Use your decision-making abilities; shift the book-of-the-month club's next choice to something spicy such as "All the President's Women." The planets will be in a dandy alignment for romance next month.

GEMINI (May 22-June 21): Your traits of intellectualism and restless drive can focus this month on enjoying more mindless couch time. Tell your children, "Find your own baby sitters in the Yellow Pages or try baby-sitting them yourselves," then unplug the phone.

CANCER (June 22-July 23): If you're crabbier than usual, blame it on Uranus, a planet exerting magnetic pull on Mars. The struggle with your conscience is only a prelude to putting your foot in your mouth—again. And if that seems like a mixed-metaphor, wait till you see your next letter from Social Security.

LEO (July 24-August 23): Count on lots of attention from friends this month. They know how you love showing off, but don't embarrass them with oddball antics. They'd as soon give you the Major Bowe's gong as look at you. Cut back on the time you spend on club and organization work, you generous Lion you. Remember, your epitaph could end up reading, "Here lies Leo, clubbed to death."

VIRGO (August 24-September 23): So you've determined, pragmatic Virgo, that, if you can't cope with elders who arrive four hours before scheduled senior center events, you'll ban them from bingo. Tch, tch. Just because you're full of penicillin for your cold doesn't mean you'll cure us when you sneeze.

LIBRA (September 24-October 23): Your inconsistency this month will drive close friends and bank tellers up the wall, at which point they'll not be so close, of course. Maybe you can charge admission. Remember Mark Twain's advice and exercise care in reading health books. You could die of a misprint.

SCORPIO (October 24-November 22): Your magnetic personality will attract a lot this month so be on guard in the vicinity of small metal objects. Because of Venus rising, tap your creativity to solve problems such as mad cow disease, dandruff or a lack of *deja vu.*

SAGITTARIUS (November 23-December 21): In the weeks ahead strive to be more tactful. Failing that, be more nailful—anything to temper your limp puns. Resist the urge to clown around, especially if you're renewing your driver's license. Get your blood pressure checked monthly and work on lowering your boiling point.

CAPRICORN (December 22-January 20): Keep your feet firmly planted, but remember what happened last spring when you took root. In the Senior Olympics, enjoy the process; you don't always have to win. People appreciate your commitment at the senior center, but, remember, if the rest of us possessed that zeal we'd be—committed.

AQUARIUS (January 21-February 19): Don't be so absentminded. Tie a string around your left ear and place the loose end in your mouth. Explain that the little bucket attached to the string is accumulating stomach acids for research purposes. You'll enjoy peace and quite during your senior center lunch.

PISCES (February 20-March 20): Employ that vivid imagination in solving some senior transportation or housing problems. Start giving people rides and inviting them home. Get together with like-minded people and write your family history. It may produce revenue in the form of book sales or blackmail.

I admit to being curious about people's signs, particularly the ones politicians leave on power poles after an election.

Play pranks instead of jokes

A little madness in the spring is even wholesome for the King.

That's an observation by Emily Dickenson. And if someone who lived as cloistered a life as she lived can endorse some April Fool's Day frivolity, I'm wagering you will too.

You can, of course, sneak sugar into the salt shaker or, as has happened a few times to Clyde Granfors of Concord, California, the lid sometimes sits unscrewed atop the shaker.

On a Reno overnighter, Granfors paired up with Wally Shelby. After unpacking, they headed for different casinos. When Granfors returned to his room, having donated his limit to the casino, he was surprised to discover a woman in his bed. That's what Wally wanted him to think, anyway, after positioning a wig and some pillows into an enticing under-cover arrangement.

John Richards walked into a bar he'd never visited before, but didn't think too much of it when the bartender said, "You had a call earlier. The number's back in the office."

Richards, who also lives in Concord, found it along with a message and dutifully asked for Mr. Lyon, even though the person who answered had said, "San Diego Zoo."

"It never occurred to me that, as a total stranger, it was a bit unusual to be receiving a phone call there," Richards muses.

Helen Deman's sister and brother-in-law took her horseback riding years ago and he casually referred to Helen's steed as Killer. "I was scared to death," she recalls. The horse proved gentle as a lamb.

During basic training some joker threw a paper grenade into my barracks. It exploded with a realistic bang and showered the place with paper fragments, my compadres told me in the morning. I slept right through it.

Ill-conceived "Killer" and grenade episodes give practical jokes a bad name. "The reason the practical joke occupies such an ignominious position in the scale of human frivolity lies in the fact that it is often practiced by men of little wit and less imagination," says H.

Allen Smith in *The Compleat Practical Joker*. Offset the rancor by calling them pranks, he adds.

On the other end of the scale are creative exercises by the likes of Hugh Troy. While at Cornell University, Troy borrowed a wastepaper basket fashioned from the foot of a rhinoceros. Late one night after a couple inches of snow had fallen, Troy and a friend put a weight in the basket and, transporting it between them with a long length of clothesline, left conspicuous tracks across a sizable part of the campus, ending up by a hole in the ice of the lake that supplies drinking water locally.

Learned professors verified that, indeed, a rhino had visited. The newspaper theorized that the animal had broken through the ice and drowned, and some people swore the water tasted like rhinoceros until Troy discreetly leaked the truth of the matter.

It was at the University of Cincinnati that Terry Whelan of Walnut Creek and two buddies toted a car up to the second floor lounge of their dorm and stashed it behind the piano. Yes, they carried a car, an experimental, lightweight, three-wheel Isetta that a basketball player had purchased, or maybe received from a wealthy alumnus. George, the player, searched high and low, then brought in the police. Everyone, including the dorm counselor, learned the story, but kept mum. George stumbled upon his Isetta on the fourth day, presumably while seeking solace from a piano solo.

Practical jokes need not be elaborate, as Barbara's son, Dan, discovered on one birthday when he found his car completely filled with balloons—inflated, of course.

A prank I helped engineer was the conversion of a co-worker's office into a men's room while he was on vacation. We persuaded the janitorial staff to ignore the change-over. The office ended up with a complete stall plus a coin receptacle, a plastic urinal, paper towel dispenser and sink with a mirror above and a soap dispenser nearby. The *coup de grace* was a pair of old trousers draped in a way that made the stall appear occupied.

And, yes, the expression on his face when he first surveyed our handiwork made all that effort worthwhile.

Good practical jokes are funny—when played on others.

Decide to add a little humor

George Burns said, "You can't help getting older, but you don't have to be old." But how do you avoid the "old," you may be wondering.

Gene Ahlf provides an answer you might find laughable: Add more humor to your life. Research reveals that laughter, like exercise, reduces stress and promotes endorphins, which are a kind of chemical morale booster for the brain.

Ahlf, a Concord, California, resident, incorporates chuckles when he's golfing, skiing, biking or walking. He's been married 30 years and says humor is a necessity for a union lasting that long. His secret? "I don't try to run her life, and I don't try to run mine. When I mentioned to her that I'd never had an ulcer, she said, 'No, but you're probably a carrier.'"

Norman Cousins, an editor diagnosed as terminally ill, undertook a study of his painful condition and found that ten minutes of belly-bobbing laughter gave him two hours of uninterrupted sleep. He made visitors bring with them tapes of "Candid Camera" and Marx Brothers movies, after deciding that laughter possessed curative powers. He lived for years after leaving the hospital. His book, *Anatomy of an Illness*, helped inspire some hospital and nursing home staff members to supply patients reasons for smiles and chuckles. It's a movement that deserves far wider practice.

"When one of life's tragedies occurs, it's entirely up to you whether you're stressed or angry," Ahlf tells people attending his workshops. A case in point: You wait at the deli counter ten minutes then find out everyone else has a number. Instead of

> Ten minutes of belly laughing ensures two hours of uninterrupted sleep

flipping out, find the humor in the situation, he advises.

Worry takes a toll because we can't make decisions, Ahlf says. Try looking at a problem on a credibility scale from 1 to 9, he suggests. You're staring into darkness at 3 a.m. with a worry. Typically you'd start midway on the scale with a 5 rating, then, upon reviewing the facts and probabilities, you could lower the rating and realize the problem's insignificant, or you may need to up the number, and determine that, yes, it's a concern you will do something about first thing in the morning. Either way, having reached a decision, you can turn over and saw Z's again.

He quotes Robert Frost, who wrote, "The reason worry kills more people than work is that more people worry than work."

When he tried resuming softball, Ahlf found he could still hit and run, but his arm told him his throwing days were over. It was like Rodney Dangerfield telling the doctor, "It hurts when I do that," and the doctor replies, "Don't do that."

Limited athletic prowess provides some advantages. "When I drive a golf ball now I never lose sight of it," Ahlf says.

He tells the story of the minister who asked his congregation, "How many of you want to go to heaven?" Everyone except a man in back raised a hand. "You, sir," said the minister. "Don't you want to go to heaven when you die?" The man replied, "Oh, when I die. I though you were gettin' up a load now."

After Ahlf experienced that most devastating of losses, the death of a child, he could in time look back to the happy moments with his daughter. "I steer myself that way."

He sums up his message by recommending that you "Mobilize your body's own natural healing resources with positive emotions. Apply liberal doses of humor in dealing with tragedy," whether it be as minor as a spilled glass of water or the loss of a loved one.

Maybe the reason kids bounce back so quickly from illness and other setbacks is reflected in the finding that four-year-old youngsters laugh about 400 times a day vs. 15 times for adults

Too difficult to classify

My friend Joan comes up with some good ones. This time it was classified ads, some of which sound too good to be true: For example:

AUTO Repair Service. Free pick-up and delivery. Try us once, you'll never go anywhere again.

DINNER SPECIAL. Turkey - $8.95; Chicken or Beef - $7.45; Children - $4.95

DOG FOR SALE. Eats anything and is fond of children.

FOR RENT: 6-room hated apartment.

FOR SALE: Antique desk suitable for lady with thick legs and large drawers.

GET RID OF AUNTS. Zap does the job in 24 hours.

GIRL WANTED to assist magician in cutting-off-head illusion. Blue Cross and salary.

GREAT DAMES for sale.

HAVE SEVERAL OLD DRESSES from Grandmother in beautiful condition.

ILLITERATE? Write today for free help.

MAN, honest. Will take anything.

MIXING BOWL SET designed to please a cook with round bottom for efficient beating

MT. KILIMANJARO, the breathtaking backdrop for the Serena Lodge. Swim in the lovely pool while you drink it all in.

NOW IS YOUR CHANCE to have your ears pierced and get an extra pair to take home, too.

NOW, the Superstore—unequaled in size, unmatched in variety, unrivaled inconvenience.

SEMI-ANNUAL after-Christmas sale.

STOCK UP and save. Limit: one.

3-YEAR OLD TEACHER needed for pre-school.Experience preferred

TOASTER: A gift that every member of the family appreci-

23

ates. Automatically burns toast.

TIRED of cleaning yourself? Let me do it.

USED CARS. Why go elsewhere to be cheated. Come here first.

WANTED: Man to take care of cow that does not smoke or drink.

WANTED: Widower with school age children requires person to assume general housekeeping duties. Must be capable of contributing to growth of family.

WE DO NOT tear your clothing with machinery. We do it carefully by hand.

VACATION SPECIAL. Have your home exterminated.

Newspapers often provide other errata patter, as these examples from Reader's Digest show:

"The prosecutor did an excellent job of gumming up the case."—Philadelphia Inquirer.

"Marjorie Evans was bruised Monday afternoon when a car struck her in front of the bank. George Baker, the driver, picked her up and, feeling her all over to make sure no bones were broken, insisted on taking her home so that he could make a closer examination."—Norwood (Ohio) Enterprise.

"Eight candidates, including all four incompetents, are seeking the four city council positions."—Cheney (Washington) Free Press.

"Mr. Brown has grown in stature through the ears."—El Paso Times.

"Studies of male-type baldness indicate that one-fourth of all men will show some baldness at age twenty-five and about fifty percent of them will exhibit some boldness by the age of fifty."—Fort Worth Press.

"Mrs. Rebecca Robinson, 99, recites poetry as a hobby. One of her favorites is 'There Are No Sects in Heaven,' not 'There Is No Sex in Heaven' as stated incorrectly in our Wednesday edition."—Plymouth, Indiana, Pilot-News.

My most embarrassing gaffe in print surfaced in a misspelled word about some Navy seamen enjoying shore leave.

Getting Personal

Put the kibosh on all that talk

"I've had it."

This was the declaration of a a charming board member of an organization to which I belong. She quit because another member monopolized the meetings with interminable chatter.

Because some people turn loquacious as the years slip by, chances are you may know a compulsive talker or two. I have at considerable expense undertaken a survey on how others cope.

"Tell them to shut up," advises my friend, Patricia. This response alienates the gabber, which, of course, could be the result you desire. But for those vocal Vesuvians with redeeming qualities, a split may not prove desirable.

"Our Bible study group includes one woman who does go on at length," says Russ, a diplomatic retirement community resident. "Our leader will say something like, 'Perhaps we could discuss that a little later; that point isn't relevant at this time.' "

However, the leadership role falls on the host or hostess in whose home the meetings occur, and not all of them possess the assertiveness to stanch the verbiage, says Marian, Russ's wife.

(". . .*You can all have opportunity to give a message, one after another, and everyone will learn. . .*" I Corinthians, 14:29.)

The most upsetting blabbermouth of my acquaintance, a man who angered people at the senior center, combined loudness with a grating know-it-all demeanor. It is one of my enduring satisfactions that I played a minor role in defusing this fellow, a man for whom the phrase "diarrhea of the mouth" could have originated.

Tom, a therapist I know, says, "Shock treatment may be necessary for compulsive talkers. Interrupt them."

That's what he does with his brother, who spreads his words with the abandon of an abstract painter splaying canvas with a paint-filled brush. "He's talking to himself, not me," says Tom. "Sometimes I just walk out of the room."

Edith is selective. "If it's someone I like, I'll put up with it," she confides as we're waiting for a show to start at the theater. When one of her friends got carried away, she finally said, "Stop! I'd like to get a word in edgewise."

What happened?

"Oh, she laughed and apologized for going on," Edith says. And, yes. They're still friends.

Dr. Samuel Johnson liked the word "bustle" for an activity he regarded as foolish or off-target. The late San Francisco Chronicle columnist Charles McCabe employed it when he said, "The worst of all bustling is the verbal kind. A silence lasting no more than a few seconds seems to threaten some people in some way. There is a necessity to fill that silence, fill it with anything that comes to mind, lest some unnamed calamity befall them."

The medical term for the condition is "logorrhea." And McCabe says there is a treatment that works, even though it's brutal. "You just stare at the person for a minute and say, 'You talk too much.' The result may be a punch in the nose, But you also get quite a much desired silence."

Betty, a senior center board member, employs the Golden Rule. When people at her apartment complex emit unending effluvia, "I listen to them," she says. "I let them talk. They're lonely. Some of them have no family around. They're usually pleasant people."

Her attitude brings to mind a statement at a workshop. The leader said, "Within each one of us is a person longing for a standing ovation."

Maybe we could applaud the talkers—then walk out.

As a Bay Area Speakers Service member, I sometimes give talks. When I spout off, I enjoy getting paid for it.

Personals are not too revealing

When you study the newspaper personals, your eye might be drawn to the one- or two-word headings like ADVENTUROUS FEMALE or ELIGIBLE BACHELOR. You may discover that nearly everyone seeking a relationship is gorgeous, handsome or wealthy.

That isn't what interested Ruby. She'd tried meeting some of the self-described hunks—and discovered they weren't. But she decided she'd try once more when she spotted an ad by a man who declared, "I'm still breathing."

They're getting married next month. Ruby found his sense of humor genuine, and so is the rest of him. So personals work for some. They disappoint others, especially women.

Isabel, a retired architect who is comfortably fixed, met a charming fellow for coffee, the universally accepted meeting venue for first dates. They became engaged, then married. He joined her church. But after a year it became obvious his intent was to charm her out of her money. The divorce soon followed.

In earlier years she'd seen how her friends who advertised toned down their independence or professional standing just to receive an occasional response. Men, especially older men, receive scads of phone calls when they advertise, she says. "It's demoralizing,'" she adds. "Either they don't call back or just take the cream of the crop."

Don tried the personals two years ago at the age of 60. "I talked with lots of ladies and had coffee with about 18 of them, but nothing really came of it," he recalls. "Maybe I was too particular." His ad indicated he was looking for an attractive SWF (single white female). "I thought I was honest in describing myself as a college graduate who was physically active."

It led to "some terrific phone conversations" and phone bills of about $100 a month for two months. Lately he's been out of circulation because of surgery caused by a back problem—not a cup of hot coffee thrown on him.

27

He suggests being honest, brief and "unique in the words you use" if you try a personals ad. I tried contacting one woman whose ad I saw. After listening to the instructions and her message, and giving my response, the bill amounted to $9.96. She had, as I recall, "fantastic legs." No, my message wasn't returned, but it's possible her comments caused me to neglect mentioning my phone number.

"Don't believe everything you read," advises Mildred. "I met a lot of men, some of them nice enough, but not nice enough to go out with." After her divorce she tried computer dating, but, "All the staff person did was fill out a form and then forget it."

At a March of Dimes bachelor auction she paid $500 for a man so filled with himself she still thinks of him as a Macys Thanksgiving Day Parade balloon character.

If photos had not been exchanged, fellows would try the celebrity look-alike gambit. "Yeah, I look like Roger Staubach," one man told her. Turned out he was more the John Madden type. But the guy who claimed resemblance to John McEnroe told the truth. Mildred, however abhors the ex-tennis star.

"One woman I know signed up with 'Outstanding Anticipations' (not its real name), and ended up paying $1,400," Mildred says. "Then she got acquainted with an unemployed woman who'd signed up for $300. My friend suspected they were charging what they thought the traffic would bear."

A man I know, not yet a senior, closed his ad with, "Yearning for the girl next door with an edge." Twenty-one women called. Following a round of coffee klatches and dates, he and his favorite have been meeting frequently for two months. "I also said I was the owner of a fluffy dog, but the ones who reacted to that didn't have much else to discuss," he says.

Isabel, who is in a satisfying relationship with a man she met through friends, admits, "As you get older, it gets tougher." She suggests that women attend church and join organizations, special interest groups or service clubs with males. "Try classes on fishing, hiking or sailing," she says. "Tell your friends and acquaintances you're available."

And if you choose to place a personal ad, remember that winning phrase, "I'm still breathing."

Time to throw away the key?

"My father, who was in his 80s at the time, was backing his car out of a 7-Eleven. I spotted this fellow coming along and I said, 'Hey, dad, there's a guy walking by behind us.' And he said, 'Can't that guy see that I can't see where I'm going?'"

This anecdote comes from Dan Del Ponte, or, I should say, Officer Del Ponte, because he's in uniform, having some coffee at the Plaza Cafe before starting his shift.

His recollection resulted from a question about when seniors should stop driving.

"It's a tough decision," he says, "one I'll have to make myself some day. It'll be difficult because I'm a highway patrolman. Driving is my occupation."

He believes older drivers should forego freeway driving after their reaction time slows and stick to familiar local routes for shopping, visiting and appointments with doctors.

A Department of Motor Vehicles phone call produces mixed emotions. The DMV issues licenses if you pass the written and visual tests. It will continue doing so until you reach 100 or more without requiring a driving exam. Some people, including me, believe a mandatory driving test should come annually, starting at least at the age of 85.

"When someone reaches decision time about driving," says Officer Del Ponte, "they should base the decision on comments of friends and family, not just on their own, because of the tendency to say, 'I drive OK.'"

> "Base the decision on comments of friends and family. . ."

A veteran with nearly 29 years of patrolling highways and byways, Del Ponte shares the view expressed by *Aging Magazine* that denying a senior a driver's license can be an "extremely traumatic event psychologically." Retired men seem especially bereft afterwards.

"When men stop driving, they frequently return to the house and stop living," the magazine said.

Failing peripheral vision causes driving problems for many seniors. Those with chronic diseases like diabetes or glaucoma suffer more vision problems. Arthritis may hamper leg movement or limit one's ability to look over the shoulder. Greater input of medication can take a toll, also. Sound ominous? Yes, especially from the other driver's perspective.

I talked with six friends on this topic and half of them know a senior who should give up his or her key now, and this doesn't include the fool who should stop driving when he's been drinking.

"Calvin scares the hell out of me when I ride with him," says Randolph. "Once he tried turning into a lane with oncoming cars till I hollered. He seems anxious and insecure behind the wheel."

Another friend recalls an 87-year-old man whose waning vision and hearing make him an accident waiting to happen. His license needs renewing in three more months, and my friend says, "I hope they restrict him."

If someone you care for experiences driving problems, recommend a 55 Alive driving course that American Association of Retired People volunteers conduct. When the time comes to call a halt, ask his or her doctor to arrange for a DMV re-test. Help your friend map out public transportation routes and schedules, plus any senior van services. Perhaps a neighbor or friend could help as a driver for a modest fee. See about discount taxi services.

Expect anger and resentment. You might suggest a support group for former drivers, or help form one if it's needed. With your aid, you'll be ensuring the safety of your friend as well as the safety of others.

_____

The mountain bike gets used with greater frequency these days and I've been eyeing a scooter that belongs to a neighbor's son, just in case.

Yes, sex is possible after 60, 70 +

"There are some men who are 80 who have sex daily."

Brenda Love stated this matter-of-factly after I asked her the question I imagined geezers like me wanted asked—"Does age have much effect on the frequency of sex?"

Ms. Love, you see, has experience in this. . . What I mean to say is, she's done considerable research. . . Well, let's just say she's the author of the *Encyclopedia of Unusual Sex Practices*, a former counselor, and before that a certified emergency medical technician. All of which, I feel, qualifies her to talk about seniors and sex.

When she mentioned the 80-year-old man, I didn't confess that I lie on surveys, too, but I did ask what seniors can do to continue enjoying this practice, even if performed in the usual ways.

"You need to focus on good health," she said. "If you don't exercise and keep the body in good shape, you can't do a lot of things." The cumulative effects of smoking and drinking also will cause problems in the romance department, she added.

"Attitude is certainly a factor," she declared. "Don't buy into the idea sex is just for younger people. As people age, they make better lovers because they do spend more time on foreplay rather than rushing through it."

> "As people age, they make better lovers. . ."

Ms. Love allowed as how some seniors take their time with foreplay out of necessity rather than as an option before fiveplay.

A strict religious upbringing in Texas made her reluctant to discuss billing and cooing and related birds-and-bees type small talk with her first husband. So what did she do?

"I made a checklist—and it was a short list back then—of

things we might enjoy doing, or at least would be willing to try once. And this took the fear out of it."

Now at the age of 45, she's done such fearful things as appearing on TV and radio talk shows and lecturing throughout the United States.

Concerned men of all ages, she said, inquire about impotence. Urologists are able to install implants that provide an uplifting boost of the morale of men with problems, but the big news is the "Muse System" being brought by the Vivus Company.

There's this plastic device with a section about the size of a pencil lead at the top. The little tip is inserted into the urethra and, *voila*, in 20 minutes an attention-getting change occurs and lasts for from 20 minutes to two hours. The product will be on the market in 1997 if all goes well.

Back when she started as a volunteer on a sex information telephone hot line, she found her training hadn't dealt with the topics of her first two calls—date rape and exhibitionism. So she started researching these and other subjects. The notebook that evolved during the next four years reflected 10,000 hours of reading, and numerous on-the-scene visits, including various 12-step programs and one call on a nudist colony.

The practices she discovered range from a man who likes having oranges thrown at him to people aroused by, ugh, licking the eyeballs of their inamorata.

Who relies on the encyclopedia? Therapists, the FBI and a few rock stars are among a wide variety of buyers.

As for sex and seniors, Brenda Love, who now lives in California, sums it all up in one word: "Adrenaline."

As a callow fellow, I confused the golfer's warning of "Fore!" with the term "foreplay," and I've been under par ever since.

Halt crime: Use good Senst

Don't tell them I said so, but chances are it's your neighbor's kid who'll break into the house in your area. You know the type. Doing poorly in school, argues with his parents, likes snowboarding on the escalator at the mall.

When he notices newspapers stacking up in your driveway or other signs you're away, he may on the spur of the moment ransack your home.

So before leaving, ask a neighbor to pick up the newspaper and the mail, maybe raise or lower the shades. But be careful who you tell about your trip. The word can circulate. Another tip: Use a timing device that turns lights on and off, thus giving the impression you're home or you own stock in the utility company.

Some of these tips come from Scott Senst, a community resource officer for the police department. At the suggestion of Supervisor Nancy Whaley, he makes the senior center part of his beat, answering questions and offering advice once a month for an hour or two. So far he hasn't arrested any of us, but we're kind of hoping he'll slap the cuffs on an obstreperous neighbor one of these days.

Policemen will, as time permits, check out your abode when you're absent for a few days or weeks. Give the department a call beforehand for this complimentary service.

"Use deadbolt locks on the doors and install a pin device or dowel in the window frames," he suggests. "Don't admit anyone you don't know. If you have any doubts about a visitor, call the police."

What about the person who says she's having car trouble and wants to use the phone?

The standard operating procedure is to make the call for the person—while she remains outside.

A dog can be your best friend in deterring a criminal, says Officer Senst. "Even a small dog will discourage a burglar." If you can't make that step, on the market today is a barking device actuated by nearby movement. Or try a few growls and barks yourself. I've heard of that being done. Unfortunately, my bark sounds more like an ailing cockatoo than a hound.

If you plan on having identification placed on household belongings, use your driver's license number. "If we stop the burglar's car, we can run a check on the items and find out they belong to you in a few seconds," he says. "It takes six weeks to identify something with a Social Security number on it."

Ladies, while strolling in public places carry the purse with the shoulder strap and develop the habit of draping an arm over it at your midsection. Purse snatchers prefer the kind with the elbow strap and in the process often knock the victim down.

"If someone grabs it, let it go," Officer Senst emphasizes. "Be alive to testify."

Put your purse and valuables out of sight on the floor or in the trunk of the car. Or you can loop the purse strap in with the seat belt while driving.

If you're stopped at an intersection and a suspicious character comes up, lean on the horn. "Attract all the attention you can," he advises. Me? I might even ignore the red light and zoom through the intersection, assuming the street's deserted, but don't tell Officer Senst I said that.

With the advent of car jacking, you've surely by now developed the habit of locking the doors and rolling up the windows.

Then there are the phone calls. It seems as though scams proliferate faster than alternative phone companies these days.

"When the caller solicits a donation for the police officers association, or the fire department or sheriff's association, just say, 'Let me call to verify it, and you can call back tomorrow.' Then you can see if it's legitimate and decide if you want to contribute."

Remember this about contest calls and letters: If it sounds too good to be true, it is.

Will Rogers' view on this subject bears repeating: "We don't seem able to check crime, so why not legalize it and then tax it out of business?"

Your style can make a difference

Does your lifestyle affect aging? Some recent research indicates you can exercise control over both the quality and quantity of your remaining years. For example:

Healthy habits make a difference. That's a conclusion you could draw from an ongoing study started in 1965 by the Berkeley Human Population Laboratory. The nearly 7,000 Californians taking part are evaluated in terms of no smoking, regular physical exercise, moderate or no alcohol consumption, seven to eight hours of sleep daily, proper weight, regular breakfast and no midmeal snacks. A 45-year-old man practicing zero to three of these seven health habits could expect to live 21.6 more years. A man the same age practicing six or seven of the habits could expect 39.1 more years of life.

Reduced pain from arthritis was reported by most of the 349 people 60 and up taking part in a Bowman Gray School of Medicine study. They walked briskly or lifted weights in one-hour workouts three days a week. Another benefit: the participants reported improved mobility.

Sleep improved for a group of healthy adults 50 to 76 years old after starting a program of moderate exercise. They snoozed an average of 45 minutes more and said they dropped off faster as a result of this Stanford University research.

Get a second opinion when your doctor recommends surgery. That's the advice of Lucile Bogue, author of the upbeat book *I Dare You! How to Stay Young Forever.* On four occasions, the second doctor advised her, "No surgery."

Fatigue, in most cases, is related to lack of exercise, being overweight, sleep problems, caffeine, nicotine, alcohol, stress, boredom, depression—or plain hard work, according to Dr. James. F. Fries.

Dragging your feet does not qualify as an aerobic exercise—Anon.

35

A three-month exercise program increased the major muscle group strength an average of 57 percent for seniors with rheumatoid arthritis. After their twice-a-week sessions, they also walked faster and noted better balance, less pain and reduced fatigue, reports the USDA Human Nutrition Research Center on Aging.

Walking endurance improved because of a weight training program for a group of sedentary men and women between the ages of 65 and 79. They increased their average distance from 25 to 34 minutes before fatigue set in. A control group that remained sedentary experienced no change in this study by the University of Vermont College of Medicine.

A one-time pneumonia shot is recommended for people 65 and over by the National Coalition for Adult Immunization.

For every hour of exercise, from two to three hours of life are gained, based on the findings of an ongoing study of nearly 17,000 Harvard alumni men. The life extension proves most evident for people 70 and up.

Balance training programs such as tai chi may help older adults with stability problems reduce their risk of falls, according to a study published in the Journal of the American Medical Association

The best drivers among older adults are the ones who rate highly on cardiovascular fitness, based on a study at West Virginia University. In research at Yale University, among drivers aged 72 to 93, the greatest accident risk factors were: 1) being sedentary, 2) performing poorly on tests of mental function, and 3) multiple foot problems such as bunions, calluses and toe deformities.

Ask your doctor, if you are over 65, about the doses of over-the-counter medication you take regularly. Many seniors do not need—and should not take—full adult doses, according to the UC Berkeley Wellness Letter. Age-related changes in the liver may boost the amount of medication going into the bloodstream.

Laughter can control pain in four ways, reports writer Barbara Johnson. It 1) distracts attention, 2) reduces tension, 3) changes expectations, and 4) increases the production of endorphins—chemicals released by the pituitary that increase one's sense of well-being.

A dramatic view of love and aging

In one scene, Dorothy, a spry and sharp great-grandmother, tells of visiting a patient in the hospital where she volunteers. She explains their chats about flowers and gardening, then adds, "He's dying of cancer, but he says he's never been so alive. All of his senses are alive."

Thus in a brief segment of a short scene comes one of the main messages of "Love, Sex & Growing Old," a play by Linda Spector. It was performed recently by Stagebridge, a troupe of older actors headquartered in Oakland, California.

The scene reminds me of comments by Leon Edel: "The answer to old age is to keep the mind busy and to go on with one's life as if it were interminable. I always admired Chekhov for building a new house when he was dying of tuberculosis."

One of the many enjoyable aspects of the play is its humor. Janice, an uninhibited tap-dancing divorcee, sums up her ex-husband's personality with this assessment: "His idea of safe sex was a padded headboard."

She and Edwin become an item. He advises her that he's impotent, but capable of providing her satisfaction, and enjoying the process.

Sometimes the players refer to acts or organs with explicit words or phrases heard on the golf course or in the locker room, but never used by wimpy columnists writing for a family newspaper.

One of the play's points is summed up by this bit of dialogue by the couple with the leading roles:

"We haven't made love for two years," says Kate.

Dennis replies, "The last time we did, you fell asleep."

She decides to leave him, not because of this sort of remark or his behavior, but because, at the age of 60, she needs to find herself. Come on. If she lived though the Sixties and has racked up 60 years, she should have a fair idea of who she is, I figured.

Kate is haunted by the song, "Is That All There Is" and feels scared, bored and lost. Her sister, Laura, provides perspective by saying that she has numerous passions, with sex being just one of them. After Kate engages in an affair with Jeffrey, a handsome bloke who regards commitment as a nasty word, she heads off to Europe on a back-packing trip, then returns. She and her husband, Dennis, establish a friendly footing, then decide they'll continue traveling their separate single ways.

Thus we learn that 1) some imaginative effort by older couples may help keep the romantic spark alive, a lesson I came across as a teenager when sneaking peeks at True Romances when my mother wasn't looking, and 2) when a relationship hits a dead end, both parties may find that detours may be the best way out.

Except for the great-grandmother, all the female characters enjoy some degree of romance. This abundance of amour I find unrealistic. For every ten women in the U.S. between 65 and 69 there are only about eight men. The ratio is about half that after the age of 85. Tough odds indeed. Then factor in the tendency of older eligible men to woo younger women and, remember, in the 65 age bracket, for example, almost four of every five men are married.

Changes are under way, however. "Marriage, remarriage, and living together are undergoing major upheavals in our society, and are not at all limited to the young and the restless," says Hugh Downs in his *The Best Years Book.*

"Growing numbers of people are establishing new loving relationships in their sixties, seventies and eighties. And the facts about senior sex are finally coming into the open, revealing the truth that sexual pleasure and intimacy are welcome, important, and (barring disease, injury, or psychological disorder) physically feasible as long as you are breathing."

_____

When my perpetual sunbeam was asked what she most admired about her husband—his marvelous physique or handsome profile—she replied, "Your sense of humor."

WHAT'S GOOD FOR YOU

Aquatics eliminates the pain

When the pain began limiting Joanne Wickman's knee, neck and arm movements, she took the plunge for an arthritis aquatics exercise class in 1992. Today, 30 pounds lighter, she sorts and stacks books as a library volunteer and says, "I'm feeling great."

By toning and improving the muscles around her joints, she has virtually eliminated the type of pain that hurts, and sometimes cripples, one out of seven Americans. For seniors, that figure, like many of today's politicians, is misleading. "Everyone ends up with arthritis, if they live long enough," the nurse told my perpetual sunbeam after the pain hit one, then both, of her knees.

So I told her about Joanne Wickman's success story, and described my intrepid free trial dip with the YMCA class, but it wasn't until really warm weather arrived that she gave it a try. Her reluctance at first was strong enough to persuade me about the accuracy of the researcher who said 55 percent of the people with arthritis are quick to discontinue, if they even start, exercise programs despite its promise of easing at least some of the pain.

Instructor Fran Scott says "I've seen a number of dramatic improvements" with students who take her course at the Institute of Spine & Sports Medicine pool. These include seniors who have put their walkers in storage and others who overcome deep depression—all because they've waded in for the water cure.

"You don't need to know how to swim and, because of the water's resistance, there's no fear of falling," says Scott. Some people wear old tennis shoes for a bit of added comfort.

At the Y, Bill Gates has led as many as 40 aquatics exercisers in summer sessions and as few as three during the coldest winter days. The Y pool, as you may have guessed, is outdoors, but it's heated to a comfy 85 degrees. Getting out of the water on a frigid day, however, reminds you of the time the waiter spilled three glasses of draft beer on you while you were celebrating St. Patrick's Day. On my first launch, I should have followed the smart ones into the hot tub and come out parboiled.

Gates barked commands for upper body work then for our legs and I imagined that from the side of the pool we resembled a ballet ensemble performing in mush. But at the end of the hour, there were muscles proclaiming, "Yes, that fluid resistance taxed us. Maybe not a Schwarzenburner state, but enough to cause dreamless slumber tonight."

Later, pangs in my back and shoulder suggested a regular program, and I now attend the classes for older adults. The workouts sometimes include Styrofoam barbells or long "noodles" suitable for semi-flotation devices. Most of the women sing along to the musical accompaniment, but I'm still at the humming stage.

You may be asked for a doctor's certificate for an authorized arthritis program. Your HMO may cover part of the expense.

The Spine & Sports Medicine pool workout costs $6 per session. I took advantage of the Y's senior rate discount.

At one of the new nearby hotels Fran Scott taught a class in a pool located just a few steps away from a complimentary (for hotel guests) array of fruit, pastry, coffee and tea. When the members of the arthritis group ignored the hands-off edict for the goodies, the hotel manager pulled the plug, so to speak.

Which leads us to a conclusion Art Carney used in the role of Ed Norton on "The Honeymooners":

> When the tides of life turn against you,
> And the current upsets your boat,
> Don't waste those tears on what might have been;
> Just lay on your back and float.

Growing up in Denver, I learned how to swim at the Y and in Washington Park Lake. I've been floating a lot of the time since then.

Relief for aching, aging backs

Some people think exercise means jumping to conclusions, bending over backward, running up bills, stretching the truth, sidestepping responsibility, and pushing their luck.

Then there's Chauncey M. Depew, who said, "I get my exercise acting as a pallbearer to my friends who exercise." He died at 94.

Maybe that's why we drive instead of walk. We sit, or worse yet, we slouch. We hit the matinees rather than the yoga mat.

The result?

For eight out of ten Americans—many of them Depew disciples—ouch! Backache time. Mine hit while I was at the sink shaving. Next thing, I landed on the floor.

I thought that Robert Orben knew the answer: "To exercise is human; not to is divine." Nowadays my back reminds me, "Not to" is a mistake. I've discovered there's a piriformis muscle. It's only a couple inches long, but when it pinches the sciatic nerve it becomes a pain-dispensing Goliath.

Imagine a thin piece of wire dipped in sulfuric acid. Next, heat to 217 degrees and insert from the lower spine through a buttock and down the leg. Yes, that's an exaggeration, but remember, I have a low threshold of pain.

For about 3 percent of the population, a slipped disk could be the culprit, and that requires medical attention. There's an easy way to tell if it's a bad disk, says Dr. James G. Garrick. Lie on your back and lift your leg straight up and back. Next, pull your leg up with the knee bent. If it's a disk problem, the first lift will hurt but the one with the bent knee will not. If you're experiencing sciatica, you'll feel the same pain both ways.

So, Dr. Garrick declares in his book, *Peak Condition,* "Stretch and strengthen the muscles," especially the "glutes"—the derriere muscles. One technique: Lie on your stomach and raise first one leg, then the other. Just a few inches off the floor will do the trick.

While on your back, pull your knee as far as you comfortably can toward your chest, then push back against your hand for a slow count of 15. Repeat with the other leg. The real challenge, now that you're down on the floor, is getting up again.

My HMO health book provides varied back exercises, some of which I perform in bed before arising. Exhausted, I then take a nap before the trek to breakfast. Of course, you back sufferers already know that bed rest relief comes from sleeping on your back, a pillow under the knees and ear plugs for anyone trying to snooze within 80 feet.

A backward bend brings relief. Stand with your feet a foot apart. Place your hands in the small of your back and gently bend backward, keeping the knees straight, but not locked. If you try this in various parts of the house, you'll spot all the places where cobwebs need removing.

For press-ups, lie face down and prop yourself up on your elbows, then lower yourself to the floor and enjoy the stretch you feel in the lower back. And as long as you're down there, pick up any dropped items or lint.

Another tip: A healthy back requires strong abdominal muscles. You strengthen them by using a Medieval torture called crunches. Lie on your back, arms on chest, then press the small of your back into the floor. Slowly curl your head and shoulders up enough so your shoulder blades clear the floor. Hold it for a count of six, then slowly curl back down. "If you're doing it right, you should feel it in your stomach and no place else," Dr. Garrick says. Stop when your tired back begins to arch or you fall asleep.

For a widespread backache that gradually sets in hours after an injury, or for chronic back discomfort, a hot bath or moist heat promotes healing. It also feels good. Cultivate friends who enjoy massaging backs or work out some kind of barter system with the neighborhood chiropractor.

This topic recalls Voltaire's line: "The art of medicine consists in amusing the patient while nature cures the disease."

The Sultan stages an orgy

Women, scads of them, lock their eyes on his, their expressions rapt and, yes, adoring. They sway when he sways, following each undulation. They cheer all his pronouncements.

Sounds like every man's fantasy, doesn't it? But this isn't fantasy land. This is Richard Simmons, "The Sultan of Sweat," before a packed house in, appropriately enough, the Alameda County Fairgrounds Exhibition Hall in Pleasanton, California.

"I got up at three this morning bedazzling this top," he says, referring to his curly brown crown of hair. The audience, mostly 60 and above, roars its appreciation.

If you're visiting from another planet, let me just say Mr. Simmons is not only a consummate showman, he's also a fitness industry who stars on TV and in videotapes, performing rhythmic moves to peppy music from previous generations. Another term for it is low-impact aerobic exercise, but in the company of his fans it's akin to an orgy.

Quickly he begins glowing with sweat, but he calls a group of women on stage and transfers it to the ones he hugs and kisses. Next he deposits some on the floor as, spread-eagled, he kisses a few of the sneakers of his workout fans.

In a group of 60-to-70-year-olds, he pairs up with a woman named Josie. She matches his gyrations, then, when returning to her place in line, falls down. Simmons, playing off the song, "That Thing You Do," quickly determines she's OK, then manages to fall down three times in the next minute to put her at ease and also give the audience a laugh.

As the headliner for the Secure Horizons Senior Fit Wellness Festival, he asks, "Are you ready to sweat?" Everyone but me shouts, "Yes!"

Sweatiness is next to healthiness, because this means you're doing some deep breathing and putting muscles into action.

That's part of the formula that saved his life. He'd ballooned to 268 pounds while in college, starved himself to lose 137 pounds and became acutely ill. This led to a book, *Never Say Diet*, a program called Deal-a-Meal, and as many as 300 shows a year at which he proclaims, "There's no one here who can't lose weight."

He advocates music for those times when you're feeling down. "Why not forgive yourself and move on?" he asks the crowd.

As we age, we develop fears, he says. My mind turns to the IRS and being due in just two years for a sigmoidoscopy. "Fears, like a virus, can take over the body, then the mind," he warns. The antidote? Remember that "You are a miracle."

By my count, 987 of the 1,136 people, all of them female, jam into the line for his autograph. I suspect it's due to his signings before show time at which he busses each of the ladies afterward.

If some of the foregoing sounds a bit petulant, it's because my part in the program doesn't bring quite the same reaction.

I had signed up with an acting troupe, under the leadership of Valerie Fung-a-ling, who's in the habit of spelling her name whenever she's introduced. She's a nutritionist for the Hill Physicians Medical Group. Her script called for dramatizing how nutrition influences health.

So Carolyn Kraetsch, Sandy Tannenbaum and I don blue T-shirts and play the roles of a body's LDL. That's the abbreviation for low-density lipoprotein, which helps keep arteries clear of obstructions. The three of us escort cholesterol globules portrayed by Linda Arndt and two volunteers from the audience.We sashay through the artery wall like a warm knife through soft butter.

Jean Taylor shines in her role of HDL. Then I stretch my acting talents to the limit, playing the part of General Vitamin E, leader of an antioxidant SWAT team. When a foolish free radical, played with intensity by Sandy, attacks the artery wall, I zap her with my swagger stick. And the audience goes wild. No, wait. They're going out to the display tables to fill their goody bags.

But the lesson is clear. Include green, leafy veggies, carrots, nuts and seeds, even wheat germ in your daily fare. And even if it's only in a chair, the Sultan says, keep that body in motion.

Another good reason for staying active—the moving target is harder to hit.

All you wanted to know about eating

You find the bathroom scale is disgustingly accurate. Or someone videotapes you from a side angle. You wander unsuspectingly into a department store's three-way mirror minefield.

Whatever the reason, you're reminded of that saying by Miss Piggy: "Never eat more than you can lift." So you start eyeing that book on dieting that's gathered dust the past decade.

Forget it. According to Elaine Groen, a Walnut Creek, California, dietitian, "What we eat is a part of who we are." Dining includes emotional, cultural, biological, economic and social issues, she emphasizes. So crash diets or the high-protein/low carbohydrate regimen can do more harm than good.

"Make small adjustments," she suggests. "A little less fat, a little more fiber, and add some fruits and veggies. The right choices can help you put the brakes on the aging process."

My choice has been to put the potato chips on a cupboard shelf instead of by the couch. Then I get my daily exercise by inventing reasons for visiting the kitchen during commercials.

That was before PC—"phytochemicals"—a key word in her message It's a term for chemicals that permeate the interior of plants. We should appreciate them because:

1) There may be as many as 4,000 phytochemicals in veggies and fruits. Scientists are still identifying chemicals that exist in, say, the Brussels sprout. They know it's loaded with vitamins A and C and R. (Actually, R is not a vitamin. It stands for the dominant characteristic of the Brussels sprout: regurgitability.)

2) Knowing what you now know, you can sell any stock you may own in companies producing vitamin pills.

Groen says we should increase our servings of fruits and vegetables to five or more per day. And, no, the olive in your martini doesn't count as a whole serving.

Mix up the fruits. Despite what you've heard about an apple a day keeping your doctor at bay, also try oranges, bananas, pears, peaches, tomatoes and sauerkraut. Okay, if you detected that sauerkraut belongs with the veggies, award yourself with a maraschino cherry on your hot fudge sundae (that's one of my previous small adjustments).

Stop fretting about pesticides, Groen says. Those dandy phytochemicals effectively battle toxins, pesticides and even the thumb prints of fruit pinchers. Do wash the produce first, however.

Add some soy to your life, she advises. This is not to be confused with soy sauce, which is so loaded with salt your martini olive would float in a bowl full. But you can sneak soy and its cousin, tofu, into dishes regularly by fixing vegetables the way Japanese and Chinese restaurant chefs do. You'll cut your cholesterol as a result. Women in Japan experience a low incidence of breast cancer and rarely have menstrual problems, thanks to a high degree of soy in meals there, Groen says

"Nuts." That's what General Eisenhower reportedly said when asked to run with Richard Nixon. I mention this only to dramatize the value of this food in the diet because of the vitamins, fiber and minerals. But go easy. A cup of nuts contains as many as 1,000 calories.

Beans provide low-fat protein, iron, magnesium and, in some instances, a reason for solitude. Groen says, "They are not fattening, contrary to the belief of many people," In childhood days my buddies and I harmonized with "Beans, beans, the musical fruit. The more you eat etc., etc." when advising others about the social stigma. Now, though, a product called Beano is on the market and it effectively reduces the, ah, problem.

Go for fiber, which also shields us from diseases such as colon cancer, she says. Fiber helps shorten the amount of time it takes for food to go through the intestine. This explains why so few people dine on bran flakes before going out in the evening. One drawback of improved regularity is the elimination of a topic some seniors spend a surprising amount of time discussing.

I've stopped eating health foods. At my age I'm going for beef jerky, certain cereals and other foods loaded with preservatives.

A quiz to bolster your energy

You've been discussing and reading about ways to boost your energy level. In the first of two challenges, kindly list seven of the steps that will bring about this desired state:

_____	_____
_____	_____
_____	_____
_____	

What? You counted eight spaces? Give yourself credit for alertness, which, of course, is a benefit of improved energy.

In the remainder of today's column you will discover seven key steps Debbi Harper suggests at workshops sponsored by Prudential HealthCare SeniorCare. Your challenge, should you choose to accept it, is to rate them numerically in the order of importance.

_____ **Thoughts and attitudes**. Feelings, moods and beliefs definitely influence your energy, Harper says. Simply declaring, "I have more energy!" can help make it happen. It's like an oral placebo.

When you're worn out, your shoulders slump and your head, which weighs between 10 and 11 pounds, assuming you don't have a cold, slumps forward. This strains back and neck muscles, producing fatigue. And fatigue, my friends, is the opposite of energy. However, an occasional down-spirited shuffle can earn some temporary sympathy, I've discovered

_____ **Relax.** One of the keys to relaxing is breathing, which also helps keep you alive. Place your hands on the skin that covers your abdomen, then take a deep breath through the nostrils until you feel that section expanding. If you haven't tried this before, stand by a friend, a mattress or a swimming pool because dizziness may result. Practice deep breathing two or three minutes a day, Harper suggests.

47

Breathe deeply while meditating, praying, listening to music or strolling in a garden, she adds.

_____ **Exercise.** Walking, aquatic workouts and line dancing are three types of activities that will improve circulation, lower blood sugar levels and give your metabolism a boost lasting three or four hours, she says. Studies indicate that late afternoon is a good time for exercise.

_____ **Friends.** Energy soars when you accompany a live wire to a play or concert or shopping. On the other hand, if you hang out with someone who sulks and refuses to walk with you around the reservoir, that can rub off.

_____ **Relieve stress.** Eighty percent of one doctor's visits were stress related, Harper says. The other steps described here, especially exercise, can alleviate some of the problems.

_____ **Weight control.** Debbi Harper hoists her purse and asks us to imagine the stresses and strains on legs, feet and back from lugging that 10 pound load around all day. "Strive for what's right for your body," Harper advises.

Studies of energetic tribes and people reveal that low-fat diets, lots of fruits, grains and vegetables and physical activity help keep them active and extend their lives.

Limit your intake of high-sugar foods. Make small changes in recipes that call for lots of sugar, butter and all that other good tasting stuff. Take it easy on caffeine as well. These products borrow energy from the future. Drink plenty of water. Also, go easy on the booze because of its dehydrating and sedative effect.

_____ **Sleep.** Try for at least six hours of sleep if you want to act quickly and think clearly and decisively. Naps, I'm happy to report, are okay if not overdone.

*   *   *

And now for the answers: 1. Exercise. 2. Weight control. 3. Sleep. 4. Thoughts and attitudes. 5. Friends. 6. Relieve stress. 7. Relax. 8. Read something in this book daily.

Especially during the holidays, I find a piece of candy often provides enough energy to reach for another piece.

Fall preview: Relax, let yourself go

I've fallen again.

It's OK. No broken bones. No bruises, at least visible ones.

This time it was Kathleen O'Brien's fault. She's a tall, slender brunette with an engaging smile and her siren call is falls, or, more precisely, how to avoid them.

She charms the sox off groups of seniors while simultaneously cranking up their awareness of how easily their actions, indifference and carelessness about gravity can spell trouble.

"Even the fear of falling can contribute to a fall," she says. Fear causes people to reduce their activities and withdraw. This dulls their reflexes, weakens muscles and makes them accident-prone.

When asked for examples of causes, my group quickly lists two dozen factors ranging from Paul Clark's catching a foot on a root to my warning about the risks of sleepwalking. You're apt to fall when you're in a rush, in the dark or in a tizzy. You may tumble climbing irregular steps, standing up rapidly and changing light bulbs while standing on a rickety chair.

A hardware store can lessen the risks. It offers a bolt-on hand rail for the bathtub. A "reacher" tool enables you to retrieve items off the top shelf with virtually no effort. You can buy paint with a sandy texture or adhesive strips for slick surfaces. Also, check out the night lights and motion-activated outdoor lights.

Common sense, one of my latent traits, also helps prevent falls. On rainy or icy days you can choose the shoes with non-skid tread, she suggests. Annual eye and hearing exams may be the ticket for some folks. (Which reminds me of my close calls after wearing my first bifocals.) Don't scrimp on the light bulb wattage, especially in those nooks and crannies where foreign objects multiply. A hand rail for the stairway may be a good investment.

"Some medications may affect your equilibrium," says our leader, who presents her program as part of her thesis for Samuel Merritt College. She plans to become an occupational therapist.

Take tai chi, yoga, aquatic exercise or chair exercises—anything that will improve mobility and balance. So what can you do if, despite your best efforts, a fall occurs?

"Try to relax," Kathleen O'Brien advises. A workshop participant who had fallen told her it seemed to happen in slow motion, so that may help you loosen up on the way down. You'll automatically extend your hands to break the fall; keep the elbows bent. Go into a roll.

Henrietta Hobson lacked any chance to roll when, rehearsing for a Gilbert & Sullivan comedy show, she missed her chair while sitting down and fell. W.S. Gilbert, who wasn't at all fond of her, applauded and called out, "I always thought you would make an impression on the stage someday."

(I'm proud to report that the last time I tripped on the garden hose I did exactly as recommended. Happily, the grass cushioned my landing and darkness lessened the embarrassment.)

So now you're on the floor. It's time to assess the situation, O'Brien says. If there's pain, don't move. Cover yourself, if possible, with a throw rug, the table cloth or anything else that's available, and wait for help. (If you live alone, maybe it's time to forge a phone link with friends or relatives who can phone once or twice a day, then drop by if you don't answer. Another possibility: a cordless phone, worn in a holster.

If you feel able, get up on your hands and knees and crawl to a chair. Use both your arms and legs to pull yourself up and sit down. Rest for a bit, then call the doctor, especially if you don't know what caused the fall.

O'Brien provides a four-page fall prevention checklist that deals with conditions in the home as well as habits that may affect stability. For a free copy, send a self-addressed, stamped envelope to Pleasant Hill Press, 241 Greenwich Dr., Pleasant Hill, CA 94523. The checklist will help you find and correct hazards that trip people up.

You learn something about falling if, like me, you try out for the freshman football team. Everyone from hulking guards to the water boy will bowl you over.

ON THE BRIGHT SIDE

Enjoying a "Hostel" environment

An Elderhostel fringe benefit that surprises lots of first-timers is the interesting people you meet.

"They're delightful," says Helen Deman, who's in a position to know. She's been on 25 adventures with them.

In case you haven't heard about the program, seniors from all walks of life gather at one spot, usually a college or some kind of retreat, and spend 90 minutes each in three classes a day for five days. They listen to and also discuss matters with a professor or an acknowledged expert in his or her field.

"There are hundreds of possibilities,"she says, in the types of classes offered at the 1,800 institutions taking part in this activity tailored for people 55 and up. A younger spouse or companion can come along.

"I especially like natural history and being outdoors," says Deman, a Concord, California, resident, who has taken a lot of solo Elderhostel trips as well as trekking with friends. "I've been fairly lucky," she says when asked about sharing a dorm or motel room with a stranger. "It generally works out OK. I do take along a pair of ear plugs just in case." For some extra cash, you can room alone.

The sojourners dine *en mass*, head off on occasional field trips and put their heads together for a combined farewell party and talent show before departure time.

Since its start in 1975, the program has infiltrated every state and nearly 50 foreign countries. Almost 250,000 enrolled last year.

Part of its appeal is cost. The typical tab for food, lodging and the courses is between $375 and $425. You provide your own transportation to and from the site. A big draw for me was the absence of exams, homework and grades. "You don't need any specific prior educational background except for a few rare instances," according to the front section of the Elderhostel Catalog, which, in the last version I saw, ran 124 pages. You can write the organization at 7 Federal Street, Boston, MA 02110, or check the library reference room for a copy.

Between classes on local history and culture, Helen Deman barged down the Seine during her two-week stay in France, checked out the Amazon and Santiago amid three weeks in Brazil, and, in her favorite excursion, enjoyed the sights, unusual animals and plants in a five-week visit to Australia and New Zealand. Foreign adventures, including transportation, range in cost from $1,820 for two weeks in Costa Rica, departing and returning Miami, to $5,640 for a three-week version of her Australia-New Zealand junket, departing and returning from Los Angeles.

So it's clear why she says, "Elderhosteling is for people who like new experiences. It's not for bingo players."

Older adults with disabilities can sign up at colleges with accommodations for their special requirements. If the tuition is a problem, Elderhostel provides a limited number of scholarships for use in the U.S. There are even some programs for grandparents and grandchildren, people who bounce around in RVs, and masochists who sign up for something called "intensive studies."

Glancing through the catalog, I came across "A 'Whodunit' Murder Mystery Week" at the Stockton College of New Jersey, Avalon; a stained glass class in the Cedar Lakes Crafts Center near Ripley, Wash., "Healing Techniques of Humor" at Harambe (Tex.) Environmental Learning and Leisure Outpost near San Antonio; and "Music and Artillery of the Civil War" at Kennesaw State College near Atlanta. The blurb on this one promised demonstrations, recordings and group singing. It's not clear whether the singing will be acappella or accompanied by an "1812 Overture" cannonade. I'd like to be a mouse and find out.

Theater lovers should try an Elderhostel visit to Allan Hancock College/Pacific Conservatory Theaterfest in Santa Maria, California. Like the commercial says, "I guarantee it."

Near-perfect seniors are wising up; family caregivers may need a hand

"When I die, I want to die in perfect condition."

That's a quote from composer John Cage and it was used to good advantage by Judy Weitzner, who said the thought is coming closer and closer to reality.

Apparently many seniors are wising up. They pay closer attention to what they eat and drink. They exercise or at least remain active. They see their doctors when necessary and even follow their recommendations. They grin and bear the flu shots and buckle up in the car. They attend classes, solve crossword puzzles and engage in lively discussions that stimulate the brain.

As a result, older adults continue functioning effectively, helped by hearing aids, bifocals and other devices that help people cope with losses, said Weitzner, manager of Senior Information and Referral and Health Promotions for the Contra Costa County Office on Aging. headquartered in Martinez, California. When a loved one dies, they fill the void by making new friends.

> An Office on Aging can steer seniors toward various services and resources that help them remain independent.

Weitzner, who also produces the award-winning "Senior Information" TV show on local cable stations, said people in their 80s represent the fastest growing segment of the population.

The Office on Aging plays a key part in steering people to services that can enhance the quality of life for seniors. With a phone call, you can reach a staff member who can sort out problems, describe how to connect with more than a thousand nearby resources, and deal with concerns about, say, the care of an aged parent or an ailing spouse.

A disabled person, as another example, might find ways of remaining at home by paying a nominal cost for home services, Weitzner said during a John Muir Medical Center Auxiliary meeting. Or the person might discover a nifty apartment, which suggests a nursing home need not be inevitable when problems occur.

Today's typical parents will need plenty of resources, based on a finding by Monique Parrish. They will spend about 17 years raising their children and 18 years assisting their parents because, even though the seniors possess their health, they need some degree of help.

Family relations may suffer when someone you love requires caregiving, said Parrish, manager of senior services for the recently merged John Muir and Mt. Diablo Health Centers in Walnut Creek and Concord, California. Deal with the problem by organizing a family meeting, she suggested. In it you may find your sister in denial and a brother seeking control. So consider hiring a social worker or care manager as a facilitator. Face the fact, however, that "You may never resolve some issues," Parrish said.

There may be benefits in becoming a caregiver for a loved one, she said. These include an opportunity to continue a relationship, perhaps patch an old argument, and complete a "circle of giving" by returning the care and concern the person once gave you.

As a caregiver, she added, guard against exhaustion and burnout, retain your equilibrium as savings dwindle, and expect something that all caregivers experience—guilt.

On the latest Office on Aging inquiry, I discovered that the group insurance plan I regarded so highly only pays if the entire group is sick.

Watch out for a blue Honda

The car I'm driving is a dark blue Honda Accord 4-door, vintage 1985.

The information may prove helpful to you because in the recently completed 55 Alive Mature Driving course, the results of my reaction test left a bit to be desired. Next to the bottom of the class was where I landed. So you may want to speed up, veer away or just bypass the Pleasant Hill, California, area if you vacation in the northern part of the state.

Lewis Long, however, took pity on us and let us take the test a second time. I zoomed up to "Below Average."

It's a test of spotting numbers in sequence on a picture of a busy street, but they hid the "3" down at the bottom where no bifocaled senior would think of looking.

In a pair of four-hour sessions, retired Naval chief Long cracked jokes, imparted wisdom and kept a poker face during the question and answer segments.

But the message was clear:

Older adults occasionally cause problems on the road. Reaction time slows, vision and hearing goes, and, let's see, there was something else, but I seem to have forgotten it.

> Everyone ignores the three-second rule

Drivers aged 55 and better get into more accidents per mile than the 30-54 age group. Those are reported accidents. Seniors are building a reputation for not reporting their mishaps because of insurance and drivers license concerns.

We do exercise more caution than younger drivers but, according to Long, that's the kind of thing that can cause some drivers to ram or shoot you in some sections of town.

After all this study and testing, is there news to report? Yes, I can report that everyone on the road today ignores the three-second rule. The safe distance to keep is three seconds between the time the car in front passes a sign, a power pole or some other immovable object and the time you pass it.

If the gas pedal jams, tap it several times with your foot. If that doesn't work, start screaming. Well, that's what I do. Put the car into neutral, but *don't turn off the ignition*. Why not? Because you lose your power steering and brakes when the ignition is off

We even talked about avoiding criminals by parking in a well-lit spot, carrying a flashlight at night, moving swiftly with confidence. What works best for me is the thirteen-year-old car that looks its age and my really casual attire.

The course has heightened my desire for more defensive driving. You sit in a class where someone asks, "How do you tell if the tire needs air?" and you recognize that due diligence makes sense on the highway.

*   *   *

Lynda "Deets"Detar touched a nerve in the 55 Alive course she attended. She described the experience of a friend who was accosted by two men as she sat stalled on the roadway. They began pounding on the windows and threatening her. She reached for her cellular phone and punched in some numbers, but never did hit 911. She did have the presence of mind to start describing the pair to an imaginary dispatcher. They fled.

A cellular phone costs about $45 initially and the security or emergency only service is $15 a month. In times of car trouble or something worse, it could be a sound investment.

According to people with tendencies to exaggerate, I leave the left turn indicator blinking during the 55 mile drive from Sacramento to home, where I make a right turn into the driveway.

And don't forget the water

Sometimes Carol Channing would tell an audience at her nightclub act to ask her questions about her life. One woman asked, "Do you remember the most embarrassing moment you ever had?"

"Yes, I do," Channing answered. "Next question?"

That sort of *savoir-faire*—without embarrassment—is what Edith Manley urges when, for example, we stroll in from the family room, open the refrigerator door and forget what we came for.

"So what if you lock your keys in the car," she tells older adults at her workshops on "Your Amazing Memory." "Lots of 16-year-olds lock their keys in the car, too."

Short-term memory loss is like turning gray, needing glasses or requiring a hearing aid. It's all a part of the aging process, she says.

Nonetheless, it's vexing, but you can try some techniques to reduce the number of times when someone telephones and asks, "Where are you?" and you experience that sinking feeling as you realize you forgot to meet a friend somewhere.

"Get organized," Manley commands, drawing herself up to her full 5-foot height. She keeps giant-size, washable, current-month and next-month calendars on a wall in her San Leandro, California, home. She also uses the refrigerator door magnets for notes and a cork board panel in another room. "Use all the memory aids you can find," she says.

> "Use all the memory aids you can find."

What you absolutely must do is drink eight to ten glasses of water every day. "Dehydration is the No. 1 cause of memory loss," she says. Our brains need the nutrients water contains.

Water also provides trace elements of zinc, and, let's see. I think she said copper. Or was it molybdenum?

Her advice: "Every time you go to the bathroom, take a drink of water, then you won't waste a trip.".

Intoxication does not do a whole lot for the brain's memory compartment. In addition to the befuddlement booze bestrews, the impact of prescribed or over-the-counter drugs can start you wondering what state you live in. Malnutrition, depression and the couch potato syndrome also take their toll, Manley says.

So if a friend or relative becomes forgetful, "Don't automatically conclude he or she is out of it," she says. Check the person's medication, her isolation, his eating habits.

While in New York, the actor James Cagney saw a man across the street. "You see that fellow over there?" Cagney asked his wife. "He sat next to me in school. His name is Nathan Skidelsky. Though proud of her husband's incredible memory, Mrs. Cagney replied, "Prove it." Cagney went over and said hello. It really was Nathan Skidelsky. But he didn't remember Jimmy Cagney.

Seniors in the workshop that I joined excelled at recollections from long ago, based on the recall of their first dates, first movies and what they were doing on December 7, 1941.

Manley congratulated members of the group for their excellent long-term memory. Then Anna May Schadler got one of the best laughs of the day with the line, "But what did you have for dinner last night?"

A cause for celebrating is a memory category called "meaning association." Why? It translates into wisdom, Manley says. All types of cultures going back to prehistoric times revered their elders because their wisdom guided, even rejuvenated the tribe or the community.

But somehow that didn't create a feeling of *deja vu*. Not in the U.S. of A.

When Clara Barton was reminded of a wrong done to her years earlier, she said, "I distinctly remember forgetting that."

Talking about taboo topics

"I know a fellow who says, 'I've come to terms with death—other people's.'"

Thomas Grimm, a therapist, mentions this in his opening remarks during his "Accepting the Inevitable" workshops.

As a former clergyman, he describes death as life's biggest adventure. "You need to think about it and plan for it. Nothing can be changed until it's faced," Grimm says.

In my session, not a single person attempts a joke about his subject matter and his last name, but humor abounds anyway amid older adults who appear willing to talk about a topic that's often taboo.

A first step should be reconciliation, Grimm says. One of his patients reached it via a dream of photographing key people in his life. This paved the way for a discussion with Grimm about a sister with whom he'd had a falling out after the death of their father.

"Write her a letter and express your feelings," Grimm advised the man. "You don't have to mail it."

But the patient, a school teacher, felt so much better after writing a first draft that he sent a second version, then was thrilled by the phone call she made after reading it. The next night he tripped and fell at home and went to the hospital in a coma from which he never recovered.

"So make amends and take care of any unfinished business," says Grimm, director of Venture Therapy in Walnut Creek, California.

Think of affirmations about your life, a collection of your accomplishments, he recommends. Yes, you were taught that bragging is unseemly, but it's healthy to find some things you've done that you feel positive about.

In small groups we discuss this. Mary says she feels good about how her 12 children turned out. Another plus: Because of her efforts, eleven of them reestablished relationships with their father after he initiated a divorce. Adeline could give herself a pat on the back for enriching the final years of an aunt and uncle with her presence and caring. I confessed that my daughter and four sons made me proud, and discreetly neglected to say it was their mother's doing.

In the best example of preparation, one woman tells how her husband described to the undertaker the funeral suit he'd chosen and even the handkerchief for his breast pocket, then she added, "Two weeks later he died."

After a long pause, the woman next to her says, "The moral is, don't talk to the undertaker."

It's a big help to relatives and friends if you prepare for the last chapter. There's the will and the trust. You should inform people where you keep the instructions about being buried or cremated, organ donations, the recipe for that prize-winning fudge. Describe the memorial service you want and who will officiate.

Grimm once asked mourners to jot down their remembrances of a man whose service he was conducting. The widow read them in what proved to be a poignant, often joyful part of the service. At my church, relatives and friends are invited to say a few words about the dead person, and the anecdotes often add warmth and humor in services that celebrate life.

Some mortuaries make affirming video tapes that, with the use of still photos, depict the person with family and friends.

Finally, you can create your own epitaph. It's going to tough, though, to top suggestions like these:

"This is all over my head"—Robert Benchley

"Involved in a plot"—Dorothy Parker (She also had suggested, "Excuse my dust.")

"Over my dead body"—George S. Kaufman

"This one's on me"—Milton Berle

"Here's something I want to get off my chest"—William Haines

My choice for an epitaph would read, "This is as deep as I get." It will be challenging to inscribe, though, because I plan to be cremated.

Demand a Recount

Time to pay the piper

Had a card from my friend, Hap L. Bleezer, so I visited him. He's in jail awaiting trial on a charge of theft.

"What on earth did you do?" I asked.

"I tried what my congressman does," he replied

"Was it the hard or the soft money?" I said, thinking immediately of campaign financing problems.

"Neither one. All I did was try to put some of my regular expenses on hold."

"Which expenses?"

"Oh, my rent payment, gasoline, food—things like that," he said.

"Wait a minute," I said. "Where did that idea come from?"

Bleezer shook his head a bit and said, "The Older Americans Act. It was supposed to be re-authorized in a streamlined way in 1996. And the spending on seniors' programs was set at $1.5 billion."

"Was that an increase?" I asked.

"Yes," he said. "In fiscal '95 Congress OK'd $1.4 billion."

"So what happened?"

"Nothing," Bleezer said. "No. I'll take that back. Congress agreed to extend the old Older Americans Act in '96 and they did it again in 1997."

"But meanwhile the cost of living keeps going up and. . ."

"And there are a heck of a lot more seniors," Bleezer interjected, his eyes blazing.

61

"Because of this you stopped paying your bills?" I said.

"No. I started paying them at 1995 prices. My rent has gone up $25. Gas costs 10 cents more a gallon and food is up 8 percent as near as I could figure it."

"Your landlord and the merchants didn't go along with it, eh?

"They thought I was joking at first," Bleezer said. "Then one of them called the police."

"Tell me," I said, "Do you know what the, pardon the expression, holdup is in Congress?"

"It appears the Republicans want the money to go to the states, which would decide on how much goes to home-delivered meals, transportation, jobs and other programs. The Democrats want to keep more federal control, because, just possibly, some state politicking might influence where the dollars go."

"How come seniors aren't up in arms about the delay?"

"I guess they haven't heard about it," Bleezer replied. "It's interesting. If just 10 percent of the seniors in America sounded off on something like this, I'll bet we'd see some fast action."

"How fast?"

"Well," he said with a slight smile, "not as fast as that 2.3 percent pay raise Congress just slipped through for themselves, but things would begin happening before many days went by."

"Maybe the delay is because of the cost," I said.

"Gosh, I doubt it," Bleezer said. "We aren't facing any threats, but we spend $2 billion each for the B-2 bomber. And the Pentagon wants 20 more of them."

"That's a lot of home-delivered meals," I said. "But what about you? Can I help with your bail?

"Nah, I'm OK. It's ironic, though."

"How come?" I said.

"I'm sort of like the Congressman who's on a junket."

"In what way?"

"Well, now the taxpayers are paying for my room and board," Bleezer said.

It was New York Times columnist James Reston who said, "All politics are based on the indifference of the majority."

You can't get there from here

Imagine you're a resident of a retirement facility and you do not drive or own a car. On Sunday morning you discover your friend and neighbor suffering a serious malady. You accompany her in the ambulance to the medical center. Her doctor, after performing a slew of tests, says her condition is not serious.

With great relief the two of you call for a cab for the ten-mile return trip. "Sorry," the dispatcher says. "No cabs available." It's Sunday. The county system does not provide bus service on the road by the center. Rather than spend the night there, you start asking people in the parking lot if they'd give you a lift for the $15 the two of you have on hand.

"No way," says one woman. "If I got in an accident you'd probably sue me for all I have."

Others look away or simply shake their heads.

Finally, several hours later, a good Samaritan provides a lift.

This exercise in futility occurred a couple of months ago. It underscores the frustration and fury some older adults experience after they reluctantly relinquish their drivers' licenses and cars. In some cases, though, it turns out we are our own worst enemies.

Take the Contra Costa Transportation Authority, for example. Its board members include a county supervisor and members from five city councils in this area about 25 miles northeast of San Francisco. Based on comments at a recent Transportation Forum, elected representatives like these don't hear much from seniors about transportation needs.

The authority originated in 1988 after voters approved a transportation improvement tax. As the agency that oversees how the money is spent, it OKs rapid transit extensions, highway projects that lessen congestion, building interchanges—big roadway projects like these. Paratransit, the van service for the elderly and handicapped, gets 2.9 percent of the tax dollars.

Here's a tip if you try influencing this group: Describe in your

63

proposal how it will reduce congestion and improve air quality, in addition to meeting the needs of seniors.

Eighteen percent of the taxes feed into the county's cities for local transportation projects. So it may behoove us to sound off at city council meetings. The problem is that one voice, in the mind of a council member, represents perhaps ten voters. If you present a petition with 100 names or persuade 100 seniors to attend the council meeting, politicians begin salivating.

The County Connection bus service board meetings occur on the third Thursday of the month at 9 a.m. Based on the experience of a friend, Terry, allow about three hours if you use public transportation to get there. Getting home is another matter.

Its LINK van service for seniors and the disabled was in the news recently after a fare increase of $2.50. Someone visiting a senior center makes the usual $1.75 donation for lunch but ends up paying $5 for the trip.

At five public hearings preceding the increase, exactly nine people presented arguments against it. Only three dissenting letters arrived. County Connection mailed 1,100 cards to LINK users. Of these, 28 were returned, with 13 objecting to the hike.

Extended hours of operation, a requirement of the Americans with Disabilities Act, caused the increase, the agency said.

Some communities address transportation needs of seniors, panelists reported at the forum, which was sponsored by the Pleasant Hill Commission on Aging.

The City of Walnut Creek, for example, underwrites the yearly $10,000 staff and $10,000 maintenance expenses for a van that transports Walnut Creek Senior Club members and other elders on weekday medical, nutritional lunch and shopping trips. The cost: 50 cents per ride.

Volunteers handle the driving and dispatching and ride "shotgun" as helpers. The service began in 1973 with the Rotary Club's donation of a van. The city bought a second van for disabled people taking part in recreation programs and purchases replacement vehicles.

These days I feel blissfully transported each time I make the nine-second commute to the office.

When Gray Panthers go prowling

When there's a protest about cuts in Medicare or the paucity of ow-income housing, you can count on seeing at least two or three Gray 'anthers on the scene, and they won't be purring

"Some can't stand very long and others may not be able to drive to a protest, but we can still think," says Doris Copperman. And they're not shy about voicing those thoughts. You can ask U.S. Representative Bill Baker. His Walnut Creek, California, office was the site of a demonstration recently against the Contract with America's impact on Medicare and Medicaid.

Baker plans a town meeting where he may be asked for details of how "The new Congress (has) worked to save Medicare." He modestly takes partial credit for the rescue in his "Report to the East Bay" newsletter. In it he also shows that, through the efficient use of our tax dollars, he can produce a two-color publication that also describes his other accomplishments for seniors. Things, for example, like the related program that will result from a big capital gains tax cut.

His town meeting comments may undergo scrutiny at the Gray Panthers monthly meeting. The scheduled speaker is Tyler Snortum-Phelps of the Green Party.

"The public is welcomed," says Doris Copperman, who is the convener of this area's Network, as more than 60 U.S. Gray Panther branches are called. Nearly 540,000 members participate in the nation and elsewhere in the world. She handles local programs and meeting preparations and her husband, Ralph, chairs the meetings.

"There have been a few issues on which we disagree, but it doesn't happen often," she says when asked about their individual preferences. "We have respect for each other's feelings and expertise."

Ralph Copperman, a retired Los Angeles plumbing inspector, heads the county Area Agency on Aging Advisory Committee, serves on the Pleasant Hill Commission on Aging and the Central Contra Costa County Senior Coalition, plus other groups working on behalf of seniors. Doris Copperman, a retired high school math teacher, then a part-time Los Medanos College instructor, co-chairs the Coalition for Reproductive Choice and is active in four other organizations.

"Our Gray Panthers Network has nearly 100 members and 25 to 30 usually show up for meetings," she says.

Some previous issues and topics suggest the group's range of interests: health care, the Livermore Laboratory, affirmative action, the women's conference in Beijing, and re-opening of the county hospital.

The Panthers explore but don't act on an issue unless a good consensus exists, then the letter writing, phone calls, comments at other meetings, and the occasional demonstration occur.

How about Bosnia?

"We haven't talked about whether we should talk about it," Doris Copperman replies. "The issues are murky."

Founded in 1970 by Maggie Kuhn, the Consultation of Older and Younger Adults for Social Change, as it was first called, combated ageism, then broadened its scope to battle for social justice for all age levels. Kuhn died April 22, 1995, at the age of 89. Her opposition to the war in Vietnam brought support from young protesters. She recruited many of them, saying, "Everyone of us is growing old."

It will be interesting to see if the Gray Panthers' reputation for feisty involvement will persuade the coming crest of baby boomers to join in the action. Doris Copperman isn't optimistic. "The group that seems most interested in deciding issues is the college age people," she says. "The in-between group is more comfortable. As they become affected, they might do more.

"A small group can make changes. A lot of people don't see that, but it's the only way it happens," she says.

Henny Youngman said there's nothing wrong with our foreign policy that faith, hope and clarity wouldn't cure.

How seniors get the shaft

A foolish consistency is the hobgoblin of little minds.
—Emerson

About a decade ago, the Pleasant Hill (California) City Council OK'd a subdivision for the country club site at Grayson and Reliez Valley roads. The plan included a nine-hole golf course.

But the developer ran low on cash, lost interest or decided life was too short to hassle with the city's permit process.

Then along comes Davidon Homes with a plan to build fewer houses on bigger lots. The pitch-and-putt size golf course would be a cinch to lose money, according to the pros, so Davidon offers to build a new senior center instead, at a cost of $930,000 or so. When static occurs about a center at the subdivision site, the developer says the offer still holds, regardless of where it's built.

Ah, but wait a moment. Senior centers are the province of the Pleasant Hill Recreation & Park District. It was created before the city incorporated and began meeting the needs of older adults

The city and the district have had their differences over the years. Just last month, the city took steps to get into the park business itself. This caused a bit of uneasiness among old-timers who have watched the city attempt some other schemes, such as trying to get a downtown started with the help of a redevelopment bankroll.

> "I think this plan stinks," said city council member Chuck Escover. Then he voted for it.

One would think after 25 years that if a downtown was really destined for Pleasant Hill, something would have happened before now.

I think it ill-advised, since the absence of a downtown is the

67

city's only distinguishing characteristic.

In the matter of the golf course, Mayor Paul Cooper said a promise had been made to the neighbors that it would be built. The four other council members agreed.

There'll be a few problems—the need, for example for nets to shield the neighboring homes, the possibility that it will become known as a par 2 course, and finding a golf course manager who is willing to go broke operating it.

Of course, as one who prefers napping—or almost any other form of activity—to golfing, and as a senior, I might be a teeny bit prejudiced.

But Suzanne Salter, city treasurer, commented during the public hearing on the plan that she'd attended a conference a couple of years earlier where other city treasurers pretty much agreed that city golf courses were losing propositions, and that's how she felt about this one.

So, if I have the right reading on this, the council agrees it's better for the city to endorse a golf course that will lose money and rattle nearby windows than to pave the way for a needed senior center constructed at no cost to the local citizenry.

As it stands now, when it comes time for a new center, the Rec. & Park District probably will need to seek an assessment to help pay for it. And you know how folks are about paying those.

Chuck Escover, a new council member, said near the end of the meeting, "I think we need a golf course." Then he added, "I think this plan stinks." But he voted for it. So did his compadres.

Which just goes to show that this council, like so many before it, believes in consistency even when it's foolish.

———

A resident of Pleasant Hill since 1963, I ignored city council shenanigans during the years of a San Francisco commute, but now I feel obliged to take verbal potshots at elected officials, especially the deserving ones.

FOLLIES AND FOIBLES

Taking after Betty Crocker

"Ladies and gentlemen of the jury, we the people intend to prove beyond a shadow of a doubt that Mary Worth has been altered and reconstituted far beyond the bounds of the Comics Strip Preservation Society's official guidelines. We also intend to show that these willful alterations constitute a fraud by the defendants, Saunders and Giella, on newspaper subscribers."

"Thank you Ms. Quo," said Judge Rimrock. "Does the defense care to comment?"

"Yes, thank you, your honor," said attorney Phil D. Ovit. "It once was said that America was the land of the free and the home of the permanent wave. It is our contention, however, that the constitution permits not only creative coiffures, but also allows changes in the appearance of comic strip characters as surely as it gives movie stars the right to shed years, pounds and prison terms."

"The prosecution may call its first witness," said the judge.

Stacy Quo called Herbert Fledlock to the stand. Despite his advanced years, he walked unaided and spoke in a resonant baritone as he took the oath.

"Mr. Fledlock, do you represent an organization?"

"Yes," he said. "I am director of the Geriatric Actualities Society. Our goal is to require, as the law permits, and also persuade advertisers, movie and TV producers, publishers, writers and artists to depict older adults accurately. I believe I also represent millions of comic strip readers."

"How long have you read them?" Quo asked.

"I started reading Mary Worth when she made her debut in 1932 as Apple Mary. Then ten years later she underwent a transformation as Mary Worth."

"And what was her age at that time?"

"About 67 then," Fledlock said with authority. "In the last few years, however, she's undergone a Betty Crocker."

"I object, your honor," said Ovit.

"Overruled," the judge said. "I want to find out how you Crocker someone."

"Someone starts erasing the character lines that reflect the wisdom and sagacity acquired with the passage of time," said Fledlock leaning forward in his chair, his forehead creased like a scrub board. "Today Mary looks like a, a podgy Madonna."

Quickly Quo asked, "Have you researched this subject?"

"Yes," said Fledlock. "The Comic Strip Preservation Society in its fair practices pact established definite guidelines."

"And do you know of your own personal knowledge of cartoonists who have signed this agreement?"

"Saunders and Giella did. They do the Mary Worth strip."

"And did your research also show any influence on this team?" Quo asked.

"Yes. Both Saunders and Giella were guests of the American Society of Associated Plastic Surgeons' 1997 convention and were wined and dined, and I know some money changed hands."

"Who represented ASAPS?"

"It was Dick Clark and Sophia Loren," said Fledlock.

"And the result?" Quo asked

"Mary Worth's age decreased by at least 15 years."

"And it's your contention this carries a message?"

"Yes, indeed," said Fledlock. "It may be subliminal, but the message is, To get along you've got to go along—ASAPS."

"The prosecution rests," Quo said with a confident smile.

After eschewing Mary Worth during my youth and middle age, I am now miffed because I can't shift into reverse the way she did.

Medicare maneuvers

Congress endorsed Medicare [medi(cal) + care = election insurance] in 1965. It's the government program of providing medical care for the aging. President Johnson pushed the measure, hoping he'd offset public outrage about hoisting his beagle by the ears while photographers were snapping pictures. He compounded the problem by revealing evidence of an appendectomy while the cameras continued clicking.

Medicare begins with Part A, your hospital insurance. Back in the '50s you visited the hospital for a problem, stayed a week or two and returned home healed. Today, you visit the hospital, wait a couple of hours until someone sees you, undergo a quadruple bypass operation, then return home the same day with a new appreciation of self-healing. Medicare covers most of the expense. However, nine out of ten people receiving independent Medicare treatment cannot fathom the forms, so they must hire outside help to fill them out, and that can prove costly.

Part B is your medical insurance, an optional feature of the plan. The $42.50 monthly premium last year came out of your Social Security payment, and this year, after politicians conclude their deliberations, this could increase.

In 1967, Medicare spending reached $3.2 billion. By 1995, it amounted to about $176 billion. This is an increase of 446 percent, or approximately one-half the increase in the retirement benefits members of Congress voted themselves in the same time period.

One surprising aspect of Medicare was the degree of trust placed in the health care industry by Congress. It assigned two employees who kept tabs on abuses, fraud and waste that last year totaled $17 billion. Bills prepared by hospitals were so creative they influenced the defense industry, which charged the Pentagon $600 for a toilet seat. Aspirin, for example, in some hospitals cost $74 each.

A hospital today is like the posh restaurant Chico Marx and

playwright George S. Kaufman visited during the depression. "Jeez," said Chico after reviewing the menu, "what the hell can you get here for 50 cents?" Kaufman answered, "A quarter."

Our elected reps seemed surprised that seniors live longer with Medicare. They forgot for every action there's a reaction.

It reminds me of the elderly, near-sighted professor who told his zoology class, "I brought a frog fresh from the pond for purposes of dissection." He unwrapped the package and inside was a turkey sandwich. He looked at it quizzically. "Odd," he said. "I distinctly remember having eaten my lunch."

Everyone but ill elders agrees Medicare must be pruned. Congress may shift some home-health services from the Part A hospital trust fund to Part B, which you help pay with your premiums.

Another possibility: raise the eligibility age from 65 to 109. Baby boomers, consequently, would see the value of socking away some money for their retirement years, keeping in mind the advice of Josh Billings, "Always live within your income, even if you have to borrow money to do so."

Congress also believes managed care can control costs. HMOs (health maintenance organizations) are the main example of managed care. They control expenses by naming an accountant as chief executive officer. This CEO is the one who decides the price of an aspirin should hit $78. He or she also trims, for instance, the surgeon's scalpel costs by buying paring knives from the 98 Cent store. So in these ways the HMO manages income and expenses and your care. Just don't plan on spending the night.

Why, you may be asking, do people join HMOs in droves? Think back a few years. That's when HMOs said *they* would handle the Medicare paperwork.

Some of them now vie for the healthiest seniors. By covering the hale and hearty, an HMO receives Medicare allotments without having to spend much. So, if you're in great shape, shop around. Encourage an auction where you can go on the block with bidders required to throw in say, two weeks in Maui or a sports car.

Now, if only Medicare could provide a Part C that could reimburse seniors for listening to the medical problems of others.

Solutions for Social Security

More than $400 billion a year flows into the Washington, D.C. coffers in Social Security taxes. About $340 billion comes out, paying people their Social Security benefits. The reserve, or Trust Fund, should now total $102 billion, but Congress keeps dipping into it, so the amount actually is down to $13.74. (Ed. note: These figures are unaudited.)

With an avalanche of baby boomers coming into retirement range, some funding problems loom on the horizon. Here are some possible solutions:

1. Rather than wait 220 more years for campaign financing reform, require that one-half of all PAC money and other election campaign contributions go to Social Security. The 1996 amount would have reached a paltry $2 billion. But, counting the rate of increase for just legal campaign giving, the total would hit at least $38 billion by 2001. If you add 50 percent of the illegal contributions, we're looking at exponential growth.

2. There's discussion about partially privatizing Social Security with 40 percent of the funds invested in stocks and bonds. One approach would permit an individual to choose his or her own securities. Because nine out of every ten of us knows next to nothing about the stock market, I propose a Quick Pick option like some state lotteries. That way, investment in U.S. corporations would be left to chance. On second thought, limit the picks to companies making lottery and gambling equipment, thus guaranteeing a healthy return.

Or President Clinton could appoint a Social Security czar to handle the investment decisions. If this takes place, require that 40 percent of the money we pay our elected representatives be tied to the rise or fall of the Social Security investments.

3. Try a means test. You probably know the nation determines its negativity quotient this way. We should make employed mean people pay 15 percent more in Social Security taxes and deduct 15 percent from the benefits grouchy people receive. With this attitude adjustment incentive, before long even traffic tickets would be adorned with insipid smiley sunshine faces.

4. Require that members of the Senate and the House of Representatives provide retirees with the same retirement package they give themselves. Ah, but where would these trillions come from? you may be asking. For an answer we might contact U.S. corporations for their formula. Their taxes dropped from 39 percent in the late 1950s to about 18 percent earlier in this decade.

5. Each time Congress taps the Social Security Trust Fund to pay off other obligations, we could reduce the take-home pay of our elected officials by a proportionate amount.

6. Change the Social Security name to the Retirees Savings & Loan System and insist that Congress also bail it out.

7. Place a freeze on aging. This would achieve the goal for which most baby boomers strive. We could subsidize the makers of birthday candles, purveyors of singing telegrams, funeral parlors and other impacted firms for a transition period.

8. Establish profit-making branches. An Extended Social Security Tedding, for example, would charge a modest entrance fee and monthly rates. With ESST groups around the country, seniors who are shy, lonely and unwanted could nurture one another.

9. Create an Intergenerational Parity Plan Identity (IPPI). Younger stressed-out workers, who fear that their Social Security taxes will go entirely to today's retirees, would trade places with people attempting to exist on Social Security payments. After three months of this, they will be clamoring to switch back again. No, this doesn't resolve fiscal problems, but it could reduce the decibel level.

10. Force people to save money before they retire.

11. Forget No. 10. Let's stick to practical ideas. How about a gossip excise tax designated solely for Social Security? Think of the potential.

After applying at age 62, I've felt Socially Secure ever since.

A year-plus in review

Optimism ran rampant as 1996 began. Seniors in America anticipated great things from the White House Conference on the Aging, which had taken place in the preceding Older Americans Month of May.

Three forests had given their all for the memos, proposals and background papers that proliferated. A total of 83.6 million man- and woman-hours were racked up in meetings throughout the land. Visions of a silvery utopia danced in the heads of delegates who had painstakingly drafted resolutions for Congressional action.

The visions began evaporating, however, when a Contract with America was posted. Some viewed the proposed changes as a Contract *on* America.

Reginald Fourbush, a conference delegate, said, "To understand the turmoil, remember that passage of the Older Americans Act in 1975 established a network of national, state and local Area Agencies on Aging, Advisory Councils on Aging, and various Commissions on Aging. These later gave birth to Aging Institutes, Consortiums of Aging Entities, and Aged Agencies on Aging Research. The goal of the people attending the White House Conference was to maintain a status quo amid troubled times."

"Did the strategy pay off?" I inquired.

"It's odd," he said. "Our main goal was to influence legislators, but they'd deserted Washington for their spring break the week we met. Nonetheless, the Contract with America has sunk into the black hole that also contains proposals such as campaign financing reform, investigations of usurious interest rates on credit cards, and a lid on obscene retirement packages for Congresspeople."

> Seniors are losing ground at about the same rate as two years ago.

"So older adults have benefited?"

"Well, if you factor in inflation. they're losing ground at about the same rate of two years ago," said Fourbush. "So, I guess you could call that progress."

"What's happened this year?"

Fourbush leaned back, reflected a moment, then said, "The exciting part about this year is that nothing's happened. Oh, people were hoping that the Older Americans Act, which was due for re-authorization last year, might be updated this year."

"Why?"

"Well, despite rapid growth in the number of seniors, funding for Older Americans Act programs has dropped more than 30 per cent since 1980."

"What sort of programs?" I asked.

"Oh, help with housing, meals and transportation—things that help seniors maintain their independence," he said.

"So the government cuts those by nearly a third to save taxpayers money?"

"That's the goal," Fourbush said. "The legislators love to tell voters about cutbacks. When the nursing home numbers increase they evidently count that as a boon to the economy."

"It seems to me if we can pay farmers to not grow crops, we could pay someone who keeps seniors healthy and fed and keep at least some of us off the freeway."

Fourbush's eyes glazed slightly and he muttered, "Remember that we're dealing with politicans here, and you probably recall what Winston Churchill said about their qualifications."

"No. Refresh my memory."

"It is the ability to foretell what is going to happen tomorrow, next week, next month, and next year. And to have the ability afterwards to explain why it didn't happen."

Yes, my job security is closely linked with the health and well-being of seniors, but in a pinch I can fall back on revenue from my seminars on curing insomnia.

WHEN YOU CARE ENOUGH

Tips that can brighten lives

If you're thinking of taking a gift for a nursing home resident, consider a calendar with colorful illustrations and big numbers. Call first and find out the best time to visit, suggests Etta Maitland of the Ombudsman Services program.

"The human contact means everything," she says. "Patients have a variety of experiences they want and need to share.

"You may find it's best to visit before lunch, since naps are popular after noon," says Maitland, who, along with a group of Ombudsman volunteers, checks conditions and potential problems at nursing homes.

Here are more visiting tips:

Find out if a grandchild or pet can accompany you. Either one will make a hit.

"The main thing is share your time and take an interest in the person," says Maitland whose mother resides in a Pennsylvania nursing home. "If you're pressed for time, it's best to forget it until a better day."

Carla Hoskins says, "The thing residents hold onto the longest is music, so I'd suggest using this whenever possible." Photos, illustrated magazines and newspaper articles about days gone by may spark recollections, she adds.

Residents enjoy reminiscing about their days on the farm or in the towns where they grew up. "You can ask about some of their favorites, such as the seasons or colors they like, says Hoskins, an activity director for Oak Park Convalescent Hospital in Pleasant Hill, California.

Focus on a resident's abilities. A woman who was a skilled quilter but lacks the vision to sew now, may be able to select patterns or enjoy looking at pictures of quilts. "Always begin at a level where a person can find success, no matter how small," says Beckie Karras, activities director, Bethesda Retirement and Nursing Center, Chevy Chase, Maryland. Be regular in your visits and specific about when you'll arrive, she advises.

The Friendly Visitor Program matches volunteers with older adults who are homebound. "Our goal is to help them remain independent for as long as possible," says Audrey Pite, program coordinator. She asks volunteers to visit once a week for at least six months. "They may chat or read to someone or take them to the store. Outings at the park, a concert or church are appreciated."

Activities that stimulate the senses may benefit people with limited abilities. Favorite foods (within dietary guidelines), fabrics, perfumes and keepsakes provide pleasurable moments

Pite matches volunteers with people 60 or better who live in their own homes or apartments, board and care facilities or retirement homes. Oftentimes friendships evolve, as in the case of a fellow of about 35 who had enjoyed close ties with his grandmother in his home state. He was matched with an older woman and in the months that followed she taught him how to bake bread and he took her to the movies and brought her flowers.

She was the envy of all the ladies in her neighborhood.

Senior volunteers are welcomed because they can often arrange daytime visits; working folks can only call on weekends or at night. Groups such as the Friendly Visitor Program provide training. For more information, contact the Office on Aging, the Area Agency on Aging or your local senior center.

If, like me, you're a bit of a ham, join or form an entertainment group and bring some cheer and variety to nursing homes and retirement residences in that way. Audiences love it when I stop and sit down.

Ushering in the old and new

When Evelyn Wachtel's husband died in 1986, a friend steered her in a direction that not only helped her cope with her loss, but also revealed a colorful tapestry of entertainment.

"I started ushering at the Paramount in Oakland," she says. "Now I do four or more shows a week in San Francisco, Berkeley, Concord or Walnut Creek."

She developed a love of the theater growing up in New York. Now she lives in the Rossmoor retirement community in Walnut Creek.

"I meet quite a few of the actors, and ushering gets me out and gives me a chance to see people," she says. It also led to a friendship with Sam Brown, another Rossmoor resident. In 1990 they found they were both 49er fans, and she persuaded Brown, a widower, to join the ushering brigade.

At the Walnut Creek Dean Lesher Regional Center for the Arts, ushers arrive 75 minutes before the curtain rises for a briefing, then relax until the doors open half an hour before show time. There's a flurry of escorting patrons down the aisles. Once the show begins, latecomers usually are guided to seats in the back until intermission or, if they prefer to argue about it, they're referred to the house manager.

Fifteen minutes into a show, the ushers sit down and enjoy it, unless it's a sellout, in which case they stand or scramble for space on the stairs in the balcony.

"Volunteers really have to like the theater to be good ushers," says Annett Hammond, the center's usher coordinator. "It takes more than just wanting to get out of the house."

As for ushering rewards, Evelyn Wachtel doesn't regard it as a trend, but she has received $4 in tips the past ten years.

In my brief volunteer ushering stint, I became known for causing patrons to play a sort of musical chairs game, sans melody.

Giving and getting a boost

You spy those long-distance runners with dreamy expressions? They're enjoying a high because endorphins kick in after a few miles and give the brain sort of a soothing massage.

Volunteers evidently receive the same kind of benefit from helping others. That's what an Advance of Health survey of Better Homes and Gardens readers indicates. Lower blood pressure and metabolic rates were recorded for volunteers, especially those who made personal contacts and exercised some control.

All this came to mind after a talk with Bernice Russ, director of the local Retired and Senior Volunteer Program, or RSVP. It's an organization that gives older adults their druthers in helping several hundred non-profit agencies in the county. Some lend a hand at art galleries or museums. Others like working with kids, helping with their homework or in school libraries.

One man volunteers at the morgue for the county coroner. "I'm not sure exactly what he does," says Russ in a tone that suggests she doesn't want to find out.

Ellen Clark, one of the 525 women signed up with RSVP, much more closely resembles a staff member of the Pleasant Hill Senior Center. As the editor of the center's Senior Sounds newsletter since 1982, she averages 800 hours a year writing, editing and, in her mild way, browbeating tardy contributors.

These are among the volunteers gaining some fringe benefits, according to a University of Michigan Survey Research Center study. It shows that regular volunteer work, more than any other activity, increased life expectancy. A group whose members did no volunteering were 2.5 times likely to die during the ten-year study period than those who volunteered at least once a week.

I volunteer for companies like Simmons, Sealy and Ortho.

Premeditating some kindness

You've heard or read "Practice random acts of kindness and senseless acts of beauty." This delightfully profound thought, penned on a paper place mat in a Sausalito, California, restaurant in 1982 by Anne Herbert, influenced people around the globe. Well, here's an idea for your own area: Perform premeditated acts of kindness.

This thought resulted from hearing about the 44 members of a Cruise the Creek Club who didn't rush their annual project. The group, a spin-off from a Walnut Creek (California) Newcomers Club, began tackling good deeds along with enjoying social activities soon after forming ten years ago.

"We'd like to help a senior who is a volunteer," Lynn Dillon told Georgia Stockton. "Any suggestions?"

Without hesitation, Stockton, care manager for the the nonprofit Family Health and Services, said, "Mary McManus."

Stockton knew about McManus's volunteer hours at the Walnut Creek and Pleasant Hill senior centers, plus the time spent, before her son's death in late 1996, as an Ombudsman Services program volunteer and assisting with Alzheimer's patients.

So Lynn Dillon and other club members visited the widow. Later they would tell her, "We found that you were not needy. You were needful."

When McManus discovered they planned to renovate the interior of her home, she argued, "There are others who do more than I do."

Tape measures and notepads in hand, the club's advance guard ignored her protests. Soon they were replacing screen doors, aligning front and back doors, replacing sagging traverse rods. They painted the walls and even hired a contractor to paint the ceiling. They patched cracks, repaired electric outlets, freed windows stuck shut for years. Before McManus returned from a trip midway in the project, the good Samaritans, most of them in their 40s and 50s,

81

stocked the refrigerator with cold cuts, juice and other items. "They even put a mirror on my bird cage," says McManus.

She conveyed her thanks one way after learning the club was meeting for dinner and a play. She ordered pink carnations for their corsages and boutonnieres.

Club members paid for the fix-up costs, helped by a generous Ace Hardware store's discount.

"We noticed how Mary's attitude changed," says Lynn Dillon. "She's more upbeat. She's inviting people into her home to show them the changes."

And the reaction of Mary McManus? "I still can't believe it. The neighbors are still talking. It's a miracle."

The club welcomes recognition for the project. "It may lead someone to look in on a neighbor who's alone or lend a hand some other way," says Dillon.

Maybe it was osmosis, but Betty Outman in Concord did just that. She learned that a friend was unable to get out and about, so she prepared lunch, dropped in and spent the day visiting, reports Dianne Lorenzetti, director of the Concord Senior Center.

At the elegant Byron Park retirement residence in Walnut Creek, members of the Women's Club chip in once a year, providing scholarships of $500 each for deserving young dining room and kitchen staff members.

Dean Chapman heard me mention my constant sunbeam's arthritic knee pains. The next day he said, "Try this," and handed me a copy of Bonnie Prudden's book, *Pain Erasure*, so she could try this approach to healing.

One of the results of kindness, whether random or planned, is the lasting impression it leaves. I remember the time I boarded a San Francisco bus, anxious about reaching a meeting on time, only to discover I lacked the correct change.

A young woman noted my plight, walked up and said, "Let me help," then deposited the right amount. That was more than 20 years ago and I still remember her smile.

It's kind of you to have read this far.

Some shoulders to lean on

For three years of weekly, one-hour visits, Virginia Eskridge listened, asked questions, and, by her presence, showed she cared. Finally the depressed woman she was visiting managed her first laugh.

"It was a small one, but now she laughs often, even when she feels depressed," says Eskridge. She is part of a group of peer counselors, men and women 55 and up who volunteer to visit other seniors beset with problems such as isolation, anxiety about an operation or sorrow caused by the losses that come with aging.

By talking about their difficulties, responding to the sympathetic questions of peer counselors, most of the troubled older adults discover answers on their own, answers that guide them back toward healthier mind sets and habits.

If you're one of those people with a shoulder big enough to lean on, you may be saying, "That sounds like an interesting challenge. How does one become a peer counselor?"

The main requirements are compassion and a warmth toward others, says Kathy Radke, Senior Peer Counseling program director for the Contra Costa County Health Services Department in Martinez, California. You need listening skills, a non-judgmental attitude and a willingness to commit to visits with as many as three clients a week.

You also will be asked to complete a 12-week training course that includes topics ranging from senior resources in the county to both the factual and emotional aspects of death and dying.

Volunteers gain as much as they give, according to Sylvia Einhorn. Like Eskridge, she lives in Walnut Creek. The peer counselors usually meet every other week, and, "It's a great support group."

There's a strict confidentiality about the people who are counseled, but their problem resolutions are discussed in general terms so other peer counselors can adapt techniques that work.

Counselor Bill Bedard of Orinda once underwent brain surgery. On two occasions he's talked with men prior to their own brain surgeries. He later heard from them that "It made all the difference in the world."

Bedard donates his time and skills "out of a sense of fairness. I've been helped a number of times along the way and there came a time when I wanted to return some."

One of Sylvia Einhorn's clients, a woman from the Midwest, has three children there. They decided mother should relocate where her other three children live. The West Coast offspring, however, work during the day and also are busy on weekends. Mother felt abandoned, afraid of going out until Einhorn's weekly visits opened her eyes to new possibilities.

Virginia Eskridge helped cheer a woman who had suffered a stroke. Now that she's well, she's visiting recovering stroke victims, bolstering their morale. This conversion from client to counselor is not unusual.

Experiences like these not only give peer counselors a glow, it helps them grow. "Your own personal development is a source of satisfaction," Bedard says.

For men or women with problems, it's often as simple as helping them sort out their concerns and letting them find their own solutions, Bedard has found. In the case of a man who learned he needed dialysis, Bedard phoned the doctor's office and was told to bring him in. After the client learned the procedure and noticed some of the young people there for the same reason, his anxiety and fear were diffused.

"We're not there to give advice," says Bedard. Peer counselors also do not handle household chores or shopping, although Virginia Eskridge did get conned into doing just that when she first started in 1989.

I give the appearance of being a good listener, but I'm actually mulling over just what it is I can say if the other party finally stops talking.

THE OPTIONS IN AGING

A revolution's under way

You could tell some fun was in the offing when Ken Dychtwald asked the crowd, "Why have you come here?" and a fellow stood up and said, "I'm 71 and I came here because I want to know what I should do with the rest of my life."

Dychtwald gave him plenty of clues in a two-and-a-half-hour "Aging in America" presentation packed with laughs, warm feelings about—of all things—TV commercials featuring gray-haired consumers, and the frightening prospect of government planners with their heads so deep in the sand they couldn't recognize a major trend if it bit them on their posteriors.

A "longevity revolution" that's under way means that two-thirds of all people over the age of 65 throughout recorded history are alive today and 10 percent of them have children who are seniors, Dychtwald reported. More than 50,000 of the seniors have reached or passed 100.

Advances in medicine, nutrition and exercise add up to changing definitions of "old." Most of the audience thought 80 is now the marker, when Dychtwald, the author of the best seller, *Age Wave*, asked for a

> Ten percent of today's seniors have children who are seniors

show of hands. The conceivable life span limit is between 120 and 140., he said.

This brought a groan from Eunice Allen, seated next to me. "Who would want to stick around that long?" she said.

Washington policy makers haven't factored in our extended longevity in Social Security and Medicare forecasts, Dychtwald said. This may cause a few problems since the first of 76 million baby boomers started turning 50 January 1.

"They wait for this big elephant to pass, then they'll shoot it in the butt, instead of getting in front of it and digging a hole," said the former psychologist who is now known internationally as a marketing consultant,

Most seniors enjoy good health. They spend lots of money on travel and luxury cars, and 77 percent of them own their own homes, he said. When the idea of retirement was introduced, people who reached 65 could expect to live 18 more months. Today it's 20 years.

But don't feel smug. Half us are overweight. Nine out of ten doctors lack the know-how for treating arthritis and there's only one medical school in the United States today with an emphasis on the study of aging. A large number of older women, especially among Hispanic and African-American groups, are far below the poverty level.

Dychtwald lamented the 41 hours of TV watching per week done by the average retiree. He said he'd like to see an Elder Corps, much like the Peace Corps, assisting, for example, the nation's youngsters.

Dychtwald, an Orinda, California, resident born in 1949, predicts Social Security will not be around for him in 2016. To maintain their life style, people that age must sock away 21 percent of their income every year until retirement. Think of the impact on the U.S. economy if all baby boomers did that.

I found the secret of remaining active during retirement: You depart early and with a modest pension you must keep hopping to survive.

Living forever takes time

Well, E.L. Stephenson sounds like he's going for the long haul. "I have had more real fun in the 26 years since I passed 70 than in my first 70 years," he says. His goal? To reach 120. After he reaches it, he'll reset his sights.

Stephenson, born on December 16, 1899, has been in the news since his book *You Know You're Staying Young When. . .* started arriving in stores. He maintains that you'll know when:

- You forget about dying and start doing the things you've always dreamed of.
- You realize that the first seventy years are the boot camp of life where you learn how to live.
- You realize that your friends are gone—but so are all your enemies—so you find new friends.

"My 80s and 90s have been more fun than my 60s," he says. "All during my 60s I was afraid to buy a green banana and take it home to ripen. I have no more worries."

He's spreading these homilies at service clubs, senior centers and, yes, book stores in the Springdale, Arkansas, area where he lives. He insists you'll know you're staying young when:

- You know that thinking you can stay young helps you do it—thinking your time has come kills.
- You always expect tomorrows to be better.
- You notice that smiles are contagious and smiling and laughing are more fun than feeling sorry for yourself.
- You go over the hill at sixty—then start picking up speed.

If you're one of those curmudgeons who believes it takes more than attitude and platitudes, you probably agree with the "Age Pages" advice that appeared recently: "Be suspicious of any product that promises to slow aging, extend life, or produce major changes in appearance or vigor." The publication says there are no known "antiaging" drugs, treatments or supplements that slow aging or extend life.

Now, before you lose that spark that Stephenson ignited, "Age Pages" says you can improve your chances of staying healthy and living a long time by these common sense steps:

♦ Do not smoke. (If, like some presidents, you take a puff, do not inhale.)
♦ Eat a balanced diet and maintain your desirable weight.
♦ Exercise regularly.
♦ Have regular health checkups, see a doctor when you detect a problem, and take medications correctly.
♦ Be involved with family and friends.
♦ Allow time for rest and relaxation.
♦ Get enough sleep.
♦ Stay active through work, volunteering, recreation, and community activities.
♦ Drink alcoholic beverages in moderation, if at all, and don't drive after drinking.
♦ Use safety belts.
♦ Avoid overexposure to the sun and cold.
♦ Practice good safety habits at home to prevent accidents.
♦ It also helps if you cultivate a positive attitude, expect to live a long time, plan ahead for housing and financial security, and find out what makes you happy and do it.

If you follow all these guidelines, I can guarantee that it will at least seem like you're living longer. Or as Mark Twain put it: "The only way to keep your health is to eat what you don't want, drink what you don't like, and do what you'd rather not."

By focusing on the seventh commandment (above), I can ignore a lot of the other stuff.

Watch out for these red flags

Let's face it. With each passing year, there's an increased risk of an illness or accident requiring that someone else handle your financial affairs. Ideally, you take this risk into account when discussing the future with relatives, your accountant or attorney. Trudi S. Riley says you should review arrangements, or at least look for some red flags.

For example, will your affairs come under the control of just one individual? If other family members or trusted advisors are excluded, they may see the truth of the axiom that absolute power corrupts absolutely, says Riley, an attorney in Walnut Creek, California.

There's a danger in secrecy too. When the person handling your financial affairs clams up, leaving other family members in the dark, they may need an attorney to reestablish communication. "This is not to say that the principal-agent confidentiality should be diminished in any way," Riley says.

Difficulty in obtaining information is another red flag. Family members, the accountant and the attorney should be able to get financial facts and figures in a timely fashion.

If someone checks the spending being done on your behalf and discovers a sales slip for a size 44-long tuxedo and you wear a size 38, one could deduce that it's time for a chat with Fred (the person in whom you've placed your trust, or "fiduciary" as the lawyers call him).

Look out for unusual explanations

Additional discussion is advisable, too, when Fred offers unusual explanations about transactions. For instance, he says the personal property inventory doesn't include certain items because they were stolen. Your attorney checks it out, making sure a police report was filed and a claim was made with the insurance company. In one case, Riley found that the insurance company paid off a batch of claims for far more personal property than her client owned. The crafty fiduciary deposited one check to her client's account and pocketed the cash from the rest.

It's suspicious, assuming you're incapacitated, when an attorney encounters difficulty seeing you alone. You may be unaware that you're a victim of financial abuse. Riley cites instances when a senior knows of the abuse but won't disclose it for fear of offending the fiduciary, thereby risking further financial, possibly physical abuse. "In some situations, the elder may fear losing the only caretaker available," she says.

One other red flag is an abrupt change in an estate plan, especially if it does not involve the attorney who has represented the client for a long time.

"There may be rational explanations for all of these situations," Riley says. "For example, it may be prudent to give all of the financial control to one individual. If so, make sure he or she gives regular reports to other family members and the accountant or attorney. It may be necessary to keep information from meddling family members, but, here again, see that a trusted advisor, accountant or attorney is advised. An abrupt change in the estate plan may be advisable for tax-planning or long-term care planning purposes or for other changed circumstances. So none of the situations necessarily means that financial fiduciary abuse is occurring. It does mean that caution is required and more questions need to be asked."

Most of my sunset opportunities will be well taken care of by four sons and a daughter. Liz, the librarian, can explain where to acquire the knowledge. Andy, the photographer, can depict the progress. Tom, now in market research, can point to places of opportunity. The nurse, Ted Jr., can assuage the hurts along the way. And Dave, the attorney, can sue whoever caused them.

Weeding in life's garden

"I should continue to weed the garden of my life, remove yesterday's flowers and branches, and foster new growth."

This was No. 7 in a list of nine personal responsibilities James L. Birren set for himself under an umbrella theme of "Resourceful Aging."

I skipped over it on first reading, probably because my outdoor gardening is of the benign neglect school. But the idea of weeding the garden of life hooked me. As we age, is this an area of neglect?

We do become creatures of habit, comfortable in ruts whose ridges may grow imperceptibly into walls.

Sometimes we must hoe the branches of a friendship with someone whose interests no longer match our own. The time may come when we prune our membership in a group that's grown dormant.

But the crux of these sometimes painful changes is in the phrase "foster new growth." The trimming and clipping will produce the best result if we try something new, take a plunge, mix with strangers.It takes the sort of spirit poet Carl Sandburg expressed. "I am an idealist," he said. "I don't know where I'm going but I'm on the way."

> "Trimming and clipping will produce the best result if we try something new, take a plunge. . ."

James Birren, director of the Borun Center for Gerontological Research at the University of California, Los Angeles, also included these points in "My Responsibilities for My Old Age:"

1. I should honor my children and all children and foster their growth. . .

2. I should avoid becoming bitter if overlooked by the passing young and by events. May my spirit not be eroded by the acids of life.

3. I should continue to seek information and learning and avoid dogmatic positions and postures.

4. I should use the experience of my years for attaining fairness and justice for others.

5. I should foster my physical and mental health. Should I have poor health, I should cushion its impact so that it does not weigh unduly upon others. . .

6. I should manage prudently and with affection my relationships with others and also initiate the expression and caring for others. . .

7. I should continue to weed the garden of my life, remove yesterday's flowers and branches, and foster new growth.

8. I should prepare myself and others for my death. . .

9. I should leave the land and its people better than I found them. May I plant seeds that will bloom for others in springs I will not see.

As you ponder these thoughts for the years ahead, I leave you with one of Ashleigh Brilliant's guidelines. He said, "Life can be good while it lasts, and it's guaranteed to last your whole lifetime."

My perpetual sunbeam and I enjoy the good fortune of living across the street from creative gardeners and we fulfill our responsibility by praising them from time to time.

Wonder where the $ go?

As you may recall, I often exercise by jumping to conclusions. One example is the senior center lunch program.

This is a great program for low-income folks who don't get enough to eat, I thought.

Well, that's partly right. Some center directors insist the social aspect of the lunch program equals the nutritional side of helping people maintain their independent living styles.

A succinct validation of this was stated in *Meditations of a Parish Priest* by Joseph Roux. He said, "Solitude vivifies; isolation kills."

In these parts there are seven central lunch locations, according to a county Area Agency on Aging report. These include six senior centers and the Jewish Community Center. There's also an innovation. It's called the C.C. Cafe. You can order a chef's salad or a hamburger or the regular entree that contains all the nutrients a growing elder needs.

In case you haven't dined this way before, note—and please don't mention this to your friend's daughter or son who operates a restaurant—the donation requested is $1.75 at most centers. You may, of course, put more than that in the kitty.

"Congregate nutrition" will devour $906,296 of our Area Agency on Aging's spending for contracted services in the coming 12-month accounting period. That's a little more than half of the money coming this way from federal, state and county sources.

Another $303,329 will go for home-delivered meals. The meal transportation cost is just $25,570 because so many volunteers make the rounds and, in the process, provide friendly contact with the outside world for frail people who otherwise might have only the TV or radio for company.

So your tax dollars come back in this direction on the food front. Some other contracted services you should know about, especially if a friend or relative begins experiencing problems, include:

A corps of trained volunteers investigates complaints and checks on services for elderly people in nursing and residential care homes throughout the county. This will cost $88,376 in the year starting in July. That turns out to be a bargain because it's leveraged by one full-time and several part-time staff members. They train and direct about 40 good Samaritans who donate their time and compassion. The amount of money is about the equivalent of one Congressperson taking a three-day workshop in Sri Lanka on the preservation of the Windsor knot.

Case managers are available for times when seniors cannot cope with emotional upheaval or they lack the know-how of obtaining needed services. The cost: $73,975. Let's say that might equal the outlay for three or four hours of tobacco growers' subsidy.

Another volunteer group visits homebound, isolated elders for a staffing-and-supplies cost of $22,800, an amount that is 21 percent of one Congressperson's annual salary.

Seniors who need help with chores can call an in-home registry and line up a senior willing to mow the lawn or caulk around the bathtub, earning the minimum wage for the effort. The total: $35,762 which is the cost of maintaining the White House lawn and gardens three months, I'll guess.

When legal problems occur, a senior unable to afford one can obtain advice from a lawyer. The AAA spending on this will come to $77,817, a pittance when compared with, say, the cost of mailing out newsletters Congressional types produce, telling about the wonderful jobs they're doing.

There also are food supply programs for the poor, shopping and housekeeping help for the frail people unable to venture out, and day care for people with Alzheimer's.

For information about these and other programs call your nearest Area Agency on Aging.

Like Andy Rooney,I believe we should hike the pay Congress people receive. The odds are in another generation or two this would attract several capable people who can't be bought.

Where the focus is on life

Starting with the concept of making life in a nursing home similar to the outside world, Dr. William Thomas has launched an idea that "appears to be having an influence on the nursing home industry."

This was one conclusion in an Associated Press story by Mary Esch that an "Inside LITA"* newsletter adapted.

When he was first offered a post as medical director at Chase Memorial Nursing Home in upstate New York, Dr. Thomas wondered, "What good is treatment for people who cannot be cured?"

The modern, nonprofit, 80-bed facility boasted an excellent record, but emphasized nursing rather than home. In 1991 he decided he could improve the residents' quality of life. Helped by a $200,000 state and federal grant, he began the "Eden Alternative."

"(It) creates a diverse, sociable, dynamic human habitat where residents can feel they are useful members of a community," he said.

At Chase this translates into these features:

Children participate in the residents' daily activities. After-school programs, a day care center, a colorful playground and picnic areas pave the way for interaction.

Animals abound. Two freely roaming dogs, four cats and 120 birds give residents company and opportunities of caring for pets.

"I love my birds," said one 90-year-old. Looking up from her wheelchair at the blue parakeets in her homey room, she added, "This is the nicest place you could ever be if you're unable to live on your own."

Flowers, herbs and vegetables grow where the lawn used to be. Hundreds of plants flourish indoors as well.

"I was not in favor of this," said Roger Halbert, administrator at Chase. "I wasn't a bird person. And I certainly wasn't in favor of two dogs and four cats. Some employees and residents also were leery of the changes."

Now, he and virtually everyone else is a convert. Despite fears of more infections and allergies, these decreased. The number of medications for depression, anxiety and other mental disorders dropped from six or seven per resident to two or three.

How does this Garden of Eden concept compare with nursing homes here in central Contra Costa County, one of Northern California's fastest growing? I wondered.

Lois McKnight, who had just finished the LITA newsletter story about the Eden Alternative, said "I love the positive atmosphere it has achieved." But its scope is far beyond the typical nursing home in this area, based on her experience as executive director of the Ombudsman Services of Contra Costa. Some local nursing homes benefit from visitors who bring pets in once a week. Several homes have a house cat. Visits by children take place occasionally

However, the expenses of feeding and caring for a large number of pets, the poverty-level status of about 70 percent of the residents, and their physical disabilities make the Eden Alternative sound "almost too good to be true," she said. Grants of $200,000 or so could bring significant changes, she added.

Pat Safford, a staff member of California Advocates for Nursing Home Reform in San Francisco, said "This sounds like the goals we're trying to achieve."

It may evolve here. At the Eden Alternative Foundation, Dr. Thomas trains others to teach his ideas. He's helped nursing homes in Alabama, Indiana, Missouri, North Carolina and Texas

"The Eden Alternative doesn't make a nursing home into a paradise," he said. "It's still a place you'd rather avoid. But we can make it more acceptable. When you focus on life right to the end, rather than disease and disability, it changes things."

---

* LITA is the acronym for Love Is The Answer, an organization of volunteers who visit nursing home residents. The late Iris Suhl founded the Contra Costa County branch. For information, call (510)527-2055.

You're wanted, even old and gray

It's heartening when you're in demand. Oh, sure. Your reaction time may be slower than molasses. Arthritis may create an audible creaking here and there. But despite run of the mill stuff like this, Lisa Solinger, as a placement coordinator, would appreciate the opportunity of placing you somewhere important. You could even say crucially important.

Lisa, you see, works for the Northern California Donor Network.

Yes, older adults with organs in reasonably good shape can help one of the 50,000-plus Americans waiting for organ donations. Remember, one of the most significant organs is tissue. Just ask any burn victim. And it doesn't matter if wrinkles or spots dapple some of the skin.

"There's no specific age limit for organ donors," Lisa says. "We evaluate them on an individual basis. Our oldest person was 76."

Based on the cavorting of some 80-year-olds in the Walnut Creek (California) Senior Olympics, that record could be broken easily.

Only 5,400 of the Americans who died in 1996 took the necessary steps for organ donations. In some cases, people who signed donor cards failed to tell relatives about their intent.

"If surviving family members are unsure about their loved one's wishes, they often refuse the option of organ donation," says the June/July, 1996, issue of Seniority Magazine. Looked at another way, about 4,000 people died in 1997 because organs weren't available.

You can contact the donor network at 1-800-553-6667.

There's another opportunity. Medical centers need whole bodies. "This unique and priceless gift of the human body provides the source for knowledge that is the foundation of medical education and research," states a brochure from the Department of Anatomy,

University of California, San Francisco.

Dori Tico, the university's State Curator for Northern California, says, "We don't rush you. Last year we had a 107-year-old, and a person who was 104, so you can see we want you to make full use of your bodies before we receive them."

Most of the people in the willed body program are over 60, she says. In the past ten years since she became curator the need has been persistent.

Your body may be turned down if you die of hepatitis, HIV, tuberculosis or Creutzfeldt-Jacob disease. An extensive autopsy, extreme obesity or an accident that caused extensive trauma to the body might rule you out as well. However, you'll be welcomed with open, ah, storage space regardless of your looks or politics. Show me a more liberal acceptance policy than that, I dare you.

Talk it over with family members because you need general agreement on a step like this. Let your doctor and lawyer know also, if you sign up.

I asked Dori Tico if people made stipulations in their completed forms, something like, "No snickering allowed." She has not yet seen that proviso.

By signing up you will contribute your all to science for up to three years. At that point, your body will be cremated and the center disposes of the cremains.

Who knows? As a result of their studies students may discover a solution to sciatica, a cure for insomnia; even a gonadotrophic. And the donors help accomplish all this pain-free while lying down.

Your family or the estate will pay the funeral home or a removal transport service for filing the death certificate and transporting the body to the medical center. My son, Andy, planned to transport me in the back of his 1994 Toyota, thus avoiding that expense. In the event the parents expire at the same time, he could use the car pool lane, he reasoned. But, after discovering, there's paper work involved, he changed his mind.

As a participant in this program, I foresee giving a center stage performance for up to 36 months. What more could an aspiring actor want?

Good news about the brain

You remember seeing big figures on how many of the brain's nerve cells disintegrate after the age of 30. Dr. Marian Diamond said the late San Francisco Chronicle columnist Herb Caen once reported it was on the order of 30,000 cells per second. She called to ask him his source. "I got it from another newspaper," he said.

Her research at the the University of California at Berkeley shows that a normal, healthy brain does not grow new nerve cells after birth, but it does not lose very many after adolescence and can create new branches or, as she calls them, dendrites, during the later years of life.

That's the good news.

The bad news is that the brain, to continue adding branches and remain healthy, needs oxygen in greater quantities than, say, napping provides. A regimen like yoga can teach us breathing techniques, she suggested. The brain also needs nutrients from foods like tofu, which comes from a food group other than ice cream and chocolates. Brain cells, which are made up of protein, appreciates supplements from foods like fish and chicken; nothing was said about cheeseburgers or mashed potatoes with gravy.

In her talks, Dr. Diamond declares, "You can't teach an old dog new tricks" is a myth. "You have to consider the condition of the old dog," she said.

In the lecture I attended, dogs received short shrift since her findings in the animal kingdom mainly rely on the study of rats. And here's something to consider: Take three mama rats, each with three babies, and raise them in an enriched environment that includes a variety of games and an ideal diet. Compare them with a mama rat and three of her pups living alone in cramped quarters.

The brains of the game-playing, socially active group show significantly more growth of nerve cell branches. And it happens among the older as well as the young animals.

"Rats who sit and watch other rats who live in an active environment do not develop the same brain changes that the active rats do," she says. "Direct involvement is essential."

When a trip to Germany revealed that their rats lived about 800 days, Dr. Diamond added another element to a group in an enriched environment. "We tried TLC," she says. The tender loving care extended the rats' lives to 900 days.

So her studies suggest America's rapidly growing number of the 85-plus group benefits from families, churches, senior centers and retirement residences doing a lot of the right things for successful aging. Dr. Diamond insists we could do much more, ranging from investing as much money in pre-natal care such as the Head Start program to encouraging seniors to accept change and be adventuresome in seeking new experiences and knowledge.

She asked an 89-year-old friend what she disliked about being that age. Her friend replied, "Being treated like I'm 89."

This is one reason why we can try changing the attitude some people have toward the 70-, 80- and 90-year-olds. "Realize they still have undeveloped, untapped potential," says Dr. Diamond, who was born in 1926. "Encourage older people to use their creativity, to awaken their own uniqueness."

Change is crucial in enriching an environment. For rats, that means changing the toys, she says. For people, the frequency and duration of newness are factors. Intermitant activities with other people stimulate the brain. Another factor is pleasure, which often hinges on successfully reducing destructive forms of stress.

We can take opportunities for more multi-sensory experiences, she adds, and I deduced that she does not have TV in mind. Instead, she recommends choosing and planning activities. Variety, it turns out, enhances the brain. The active participant also needs some time to be alone, she says.

Dr. Diamond, who joined UC nearly 40 years ago, is the author of *Enriching Your Heredity*, articles galore, and the winner of many teaching awards. She quotes a former professor who, after learning the results of one of her breakthrough studies, observed, "He who lives with his wits dies with his wits."

Dr. Diamond also quotes Emerson: "We don't count a man's years until he has nothing left to count."

Take time to talk it over

Nearly ten years ago, Dr. Nancy Snyderman was talking to a surgeon from Germany and he said, "You Americans are the only people who think dying is an option."

She cites this perceptive gem while deploring our reluctance to talk about difficult subjects like death and dying. Her grandmother, for example, often said things like, "If I die, I want you to have the picture over the mantelpiece." Her daughter would then reply, "What do you mean, *if* you die. . .

Like so many of the rest of us, she couldn't bring herself to saying, "*When* I die. . ."

Dr. Snyderman, a regular on "Good Morning America" and "Prime Time Live," offers one theory why we put off crucial discussions. "We love crisis management. It gives us stuff to do and makes us the focus of attention."

Then she adds: "It's the dumbest approach to living you can have."

Our reticence is just as bad as a generation ago, she believes.

Her mother, however, chose a Christmas holiday to try something different. Dr. Snyderman and her sister and brother learned that all of their parents' beautiful antique furniture was up for grabs. The trio received different colored Post-its with instructions to place one on each piece they wanted after their parents died.

Dr. Snyderman, a bit nonplused about the assignment at Christmas time, nonetheless showered the place with her Post-its. Her siblings, though, couldn't cope with this "ghoulish" task. A few years later, when the parents moved to a much smaller place, she became the owner of all the furniture.

"My mother made me promise to share it with the others, if they really wanted it," she recalls.

If your family history reveals a recurring disease, you need to "head it off at the pass" with annual check-ups and tests. For Dr. Snyderman, the threat is colon cancer, which claimed her grandfather and required an operation for her father. "I time the screenings around my birthday so I won't forget."

Enlist your doctor in discussions about your own death and dying, says Dr. Snyderman, who continues part-time with her practice, writes articles and books, and does segments on CBS radio's "Healthtalk."

"Doctors are terrible about inviting this discussion," she admits. So the patient must spell out the type of treatment desired, where it should be given, and the quality of life objectives in the event of a deadly illness or accident.

"You and the doctor need a good relationship, one of mutual respect and communication," she says. Your doctor should have a copy of your durable power of attorney

Relations erode at times because of time limits in managed care or the absence of a private doctor. Women ignore or skip the news that one out of two women will die of heart disease. Because men die earlier with heart problems, the news focuses on them.

On the plus side, tests of estrogen replacement therapy indicates it can make a difference for women in reducing heart disease risks. It's also good for bones and, based on preliminary tests, may diminish the effects or delay Alzheimer's disease, she says.

Her friend, Susan Love, encourages women to start taking estrogen at around age 60. This lessens the already slight risk of breast cancer because of estrogen while also helping the heart.

Both women and men must take calcium as habitually as brushing their teeth, Dr. Snyderman insists, adding that osteoporosis is a preventable illness. Add to this ample amounts of green vegetables, skim milk and dairy products. Walking, running, bicycling and other weight-bearing exercises also are vital.

"We've stopped talking to each other," says Dr. Snyderman. "Families don't discuss things. Everyone's on the run."

Communication is the way we can come to grips with life, death, sex and other crucial matters. Dealing with realities can give us and, especially, youngsters ability to deal with reality.

"This is a gift we can give them," she says.

A. A. Milne maintained, "The art of giving presents is to give-something which others cannot buy for themselves."

Extending the years

Attend church regularly. Try a totally new, intellectually stimulating activity. Get off the couch and exercise. Cut your food intake in half.

These are just a few of the things you might encourage your spouse or special friend to do because these steps can extend and enhance their mature years, based on some recent reports.

Peter Jennings, for example, cited on his ABC newscast a study showing that faithful church goers, on average, live longer.

And, no, this was not followed by some wag saying, "It just seems longer."

There was a lot of excitement at the latest senior lunch at my church. Our speaker announced that there are 672 different kinds of sin. She's been besieged by requests for the list, mostly from people who think they may have missed something.

As for stimulating the brain cells, Lynne Lamberg describes a woman in her 40s who started studying piano. A number of years later, the woman visited Italy and quickly picked up enough of the language to converse with natives. She wondered if the piano study helped.

Yes, indeed. There's a mental bonus from taking up a totally new activity and striving to link new information to what you already know, Lamberg says in the July/August, 1997, issue of New Choices Magazine

Her article also quotes Dr. Timothy Monk on the benefits of a 20-30 minute afternoon nap for the 50 and better crowd. Dr. Monk heads the University of Pittsburgh's Human Chronobiology Research Center. He says, "Mornings are best for your most mentally challenging tasks."

So take on new challenges, keep abreast of research and get adequate sleep, says Lamberg, the author of *Body Rhythms, Chronobiology and Peak Performance*. There's another perk if you can enjoy the process. A Harvard study shows that people who feel good about themselves stay sharper longer.

For a readable, comprehensive article on aging, find a copy of the November, 1997, National Geographic. Author Rick Weiss visited medical centers and universities that conduct studies on the subject. Some highlights:

Reducing the caloric intake of lab mice by 60 percent doubles their life span. University of Wisconsin-Madison studies have not included many people but they suggest we could live longer, develop stronger immune systems and delay the incidence of cancer, diabetes and other ailments by reducing our fat intake and eating more fruits and vegetables. Weiss concludes that the hunger factor will keep most people from slashing their diets even 30 percent.

Even 90-year-old weaklings can regain the strength and vitality they enjoyed at age 60 with simple exercises in and around their own homes, reports the U.S. Department of Agriculture's Human Nutrition Research Center on Aging in Boston. "Much of what we think of as aging is really just a by-product of inactivity and poor nutrition," says Miriam Nelson, a department physiologist. A moderate amount of exercise induces anti-aging mechanisms scientists strive for with hormones, gene manipulation and caloric cuts.

The "Use it or lose it" aphorism applies to the brain as well as the body. Adults who keep reading, learning and interacting with others will maintain memory and stand a better chance of avoiding senility than "those who retreat into themselves," Weiss says.

Social and psychological factors in aging are important according to long-range studies of nuns in the School Sisters of Notre Dame, a convent in rural Mankato, Minnesota. "Studies have shown that seniors who have emotional support from friends and family have lower levels of stress hormones circulating in their blood and are less likely to die in the near future than are those who feel lonely and isolated," Weiss says. Health also is enhanced by giving and sharing.

It appears that the retiree got it right when he said, "Age is a matter of attitude. I'm retreaded, not retired."

CARES AND CONCERNS

If you can't laugh, you cry

"Is it better to do what she wants me to do, or is it better to do what I think should be done?"

This was a question posed in the narrow confines of a Grace Presbyterian Church room where the group of male caregivers meets on the second and fourth Wednesdays of the month.

"Tell her yes, then do what you think is best," said a man whose wife has Alzheimer's. The wives of most of the 11 men present suffer from some form of dementia.

The men typically spend an hour-and-a-half together comparing notes on everything from prescriptions to cooking a casserole. Ken Salonen, a social worker, is called the facilitator, but, based on the interchange in a pair of sessions I attended, the word "friend" would be closer to the mark.

Dick came up with an idea for a booklet written ". . .to be a guide to you in your efforts to take over some of the duties that you so eagerly let your wife do." And as testimony to the demanding aspects of caregiving, he's missed meetings lately, recuperating from a heart attack.

The booklet includes a lot of pages only one-third or one-half filled, but there are tips for cookbooks plus ideas from *Hints, Tips and Empty Wisdom* by Heloise. Page 1 begins: "The KISS approach of Keep It Simple, Stupid was never more kindlier said than for the beginning cook."

The personal care section deals with bathing, helping one's

105

wife with toilet use, and buying clothing. For bras, the advice is, "Take in an old one and let the salesperson figure it out." Which strikes me as Solomon-like in its wisdom.

Ed commented about the challenge when "You start doing things yourself that your wife used to do for you." Even more challenging is the time when she stands for an hour before the closet trying to decide what to wear or her expression when she pauses in the kitchen and asks, "How do you bake a potato?"

During the time these men gather they can leave their wives next door in the church's multi-use room, also provided at no charge, where staff members of the co-sponsoring Diablo Respite Center conduct activities.

Salonen, a member of the Geriatric Outreach of the Contra Costa County's Health Plan near San Francisco, has participated since the group formed nearly five years ago. It is the only men's support group in the county. He says, "I'm humbled by all this; that I can facilitate some of this interchange. They keep coming back. Even ones whose wives have died come back. They find the group a comfortable place to express their grief."

"Caregiving takes all your time," one man says. "There's less control."

"You find you didn't have as much as you thought you did."

As for Alzheimer's, "I don't think in our lifetime they'll come up with something that'll prevent it," says Ned.

"It's like AIDS," his neighbor says. "There're are some things that help, but no cure."

Ed says, "With most other illnesses you have your mind. Not with this."

"They stop being people."

"You wonder why."

"It doesn't make sense."

"At first she wanted to die," says Ed. "Now, the depression is gone, and she wants to live."

The talk is candid, the pain palpable. Then comes a degree of relief. Lou reads one of bits of doggerel. There is laughter.

"You need to laugh," the man next to me confides. "Otherwise you cry."

A quandary for the disabled

At times he must feel like Don Quixote flailing away at endless windmills along the horizon, but Elvis Bozarth doesn't think of saying, "Whoa."

His daughter, Kathy, was born mentally retarded. Like many developmentally disabled people and the public at large, she benefited from improved medical care and nutrition, plus exercise.

"We didn't think they would ever grow old," Bozarth, a retired minister, says of this special younger generation. Now, however, as increasing numbers of disabled people reach retirement age, Bozarth and others are spying needs that legislation could address.

"The concept has grown for services so people can age in place and stay at home," he says. "The same idea exists for people with developmental disabilities, but they can't find the funds."

That's why Bozarth continues his travels around California amid his appearance as a guest lecturer for Sonoma State University's Gerontology Department. He wants people who will advocate for legislative change and volunteer as well.

He describes his mission within a narrow time frame, which reminds him that "At my first church I gave what I thought was a scintillating sermon and an older pastor came up later and put his arm around my shoulder and he said, 'Remember, Elvis, for your message to be immortal doesn't mean that it has to be eternal.'"

> **A search for advocates and volunters**

He hopes one day to see a retirement program patterned after supported employment programs like the Concord (California) Commercial Support Services where developmentally disabled people work. In programs like this, they should be able to set aside part of the money received from SSI or earnings and use it for retirement, Bozarth contends. As it stands now, earnings above a certain level cause a reduction in SSI payments.

"It would be like an IRA," he says.

Half a dozen seniors are among the 85 clients working at Commercial Support Services. The average wage for someone who prepares mailings, package items and shrink wraps products is $77 a month, says David Duart, CSS program director. This is for a workday from 9 a.m. to 2:45 p.m.

Another 44 developmentally disabled clients are with outside firms, but can still benefit from the individualized CSS help with social, living and self-help skills.

"We see lives beginning to change," says Duart. "Clients begin arriving on public transportation and some can move to a board and care facility or an apartment. For many, this program is the center of their social lives."

"We have trips to the malls, coffee hours and community activities," says Donna Mann, adult programs supervisor. "Efforts to tie in with senior center activities haven't panned out because the times don't coincide with our 9:30 to 3:30 schedule."

These are programs Elvis Bozarth would have praised, had he the time for a visit, but he was headed elsewhere, spear in hand, looking for a few good advocates, volunteers and windmills.

Like the woodpecker, people like Elvis Bozarth keep pecking away until they complete the work they started.

Care managers in jeopardy

"Maybe you can help this man," the receptionist told Linda Scanlin in a tone that was almost a plea.

Scanlin trudged up to the front desk of the Walnut Creek (California) Senior Club, then listened to a long message from a man who claimed he'd originated a slogan that was better than sliced bread.

"You got your pencil handy, young lady?" he declared. "Well, here it is:

"YOU BETTER WATCH OUT, WE'VE GOT CLOUT."

Scanlin wished him well, rolled her eyes at the receptionist and resumed her work. She pitched the message, but—and here we give credit to the power of sloganizing—the words stuck, sort of like that piece of plastic wrap that clings to you despite repeated flips of the wrist.

She described the encounter shortly after I'd heard some words that cling. Karen Gee of the Family and Community Services told what lies ahead for the most vulnerable elderly because of United Way's decision to discontinue funding for the nonprofit agency's care managers. A staff of five will be reduced to one.

A care manager is the person who visits the elderly woman who is disoriented, finds out about her lifestyle, eating habits and medications, and arranges for help. The care manager visits an older couple whose problem includes a husband who is a verbally abusive souse and, after some delicate persuasion, gets them to a counselor at a college where the advice is nominal in cost. A care manager at a senior center counsels a woman whose daughter has died and helps with the funeral arrangements, then lines her up with a support group even as she assuages the grief of a woman now without any living relatives.

These people with problems do not have much in the way of clout. Without assistance, they often end up in the emergency rooms of hospitals or in nursing homes or just give up.

"The care manager is the linchpin," said Judy Weitzner of the county Office on Aging. People dial its "one-stop" phone number, looking for help for their own needs and the needs of others. With only one

109

care manager in the county, some troubled people will, to use that all-too-graphic phrase, fall through the cracks.

United Way, as you'll recall, was belted hard when its national director got caught using donated money for a lifestyle like a movie star. As a result, lots of people started giving their money to other causes. The organization has altered its objectives in passing along contributions to other agencies. Even the Salvation Army was cut off.

The United Way switch is just one blip on the screen. California wants to decrease support to the elderly and disabled. Proposed federal legislation would pull the rug from many people least able to fend for themselves. County programs such as geriatric services are being emasculated. Even HMOs now limit their care managers to one visit per member, and one visit for a troubled senior just won't cut it, the experts say.

Consider this: Americans could realize a health-cost savings of more than $5 billion a year by delaying for only one month the nursing home placement of older adults. That's the estimate in a National Academy of Science report called "Extending Life, Enhancing Life."

We possess this talent for creating worthwhile programs, then, as they reach their goals, we lop off the dollars, oblivious to the fact that problems down the road will cost far more to solve.

Gray Panther Ralph Copperman emphasized that, amidst these imbroglios, we pay for the savings and loan debacle, corporate profits are up and corporate taxes are down. The U.S. Census Bureau says that without security programs, 48 percent of America's seniors would fall under the poverty line, according to Aging Today editor Paul Kleyman.

Copperman said that some day seniors might get fed up enough to rant a bit in picket lines or in protest marches. Who knows? Maybe clout will out.

Maybe that crooked United Way CEO really took to heart Francis Bacon's maxim: "Money is like muck, not good except it be spread."

Another view on your security

More teenagers believe in flying saucers than in the likelihood of Social Security still operating when they retire.

Horace Deets mentions the survey that produced this response in his talks. It's part of the gloom and doom mood about current trends as the next century approaches, says the executive director of the American Association of Retired People. Coupled with this, "I notice in this country a growing cynicism and mistrust of anything big—in particular, government," he adds. A diminishing number of people seem to believe government is working in their best interest.

Predictions for Social Security include words like "crisis" and "on the verge of bankruptcy," Deets says. Giving the subject perspective, he reminds the meeting I'm attending that before 1935, from 35 to 40 percent of the people over the age of 65 lived below the poverty level. Today, thanks to the program and its disability coverage and survivors' benefits, the level is 12.9 percent.

Although "That's a tremendous improvement. . .It's still too many," he says. "But the important part to keep in mind is that Social Security currently generates more revenue than it pays out. It is building a surplus." This will continue through 2015 when it will reach $3.1 trillion. That reserve will taper off as the baby boomers retire. Social Security is actuarially solid until 2030.

"If it were to make a 2 percent adjustment, we could probably make it solvent for 75 years," says Deets. "Very little around this country has that kind of financial security."

> A 2 percent adjustment could keep it solvent.

Nonetheless, skepticism remains. Ideas such as privatizing Social Security crop up. And what does privatizing involve?

"Instead of putting it (your money) into a central fund like it's done now. . ." Deets says, "we'll give everybody the money. You go out and invest it on your own, and you'll get a better return on your investment.

"Some people might live in Orange County," he said, recalling a treasurer whose investment ideas resulted in bankruptcy. "They may need the money on a day when the stock market's down, and there's not an opportunity to buy low and sell high."

He isn't knocking the stock market. But he asks the audience to remember Social Security's main principles: It is universal. All who work have a right to it. It's established because we've earned wages. Our benefit is a combination of years worked and contributions made, not how much we possess in retirement. It's an income transfer program. Yes, people with higher wages get more money back, but lower-income people get a higher replacement rate of their salary when they receive benefits. Everybody contributes and everybody gets something back. "It has provided stability in society by being a solid floor for economic security in retirement," he says.

Emphasizing his hopes for his 30-year-old son, Deets says, "I'm very concerned that he has adequate income security and health care in his retirement, and I want the same for my grandson. I think all of you want the same thing. This is not a question of one generation trying to take to deprive another generation. If we work creatively with a sense of vision, there's no reason why we can't have that bright future, not only for ourselves but for others."

Politicians are ducking Social Security and Medicare issues, Deets says. The Medicare trust fund normally has a ten year "window of solvency," or reserve. Some of that reserve had to be tapped in 1996. The shortfall could have been fixed with $110 billion the previous year. A solution will run about $150 billion, if it's addressed at all.

But Horace Deets remains optimistic. "I think the American know-how and Yankee ingenuity will be more than enough to take on the problems we will be facing," he concludes.

I feel confident about the system even though it's the government telling me, "Your check is in the mail."

Take care if you're a caregiver

The woman's husband suffered from Lou Gehrig's disease. She was caring for him seven days a week and confided that she couldn't spare the money for in-home help.

Wendy Lustbader persuaded her that a few hours of respite was feasible with a $5 an hour aide. Next, to assuage her guilt, Lustbader, in her role as a social worker in Seattle, talked with the woman's husband. "This is a chance for you to give your wife the gift of a few hours of rest," she said. "Kick her out." He nodded in agreement.

But how to spend those hours? "You forget what it is to have a life," the woman said. Then she recalled her walking club and, with some urging, found that the members still met at the donut shop. And, if it was raining, they still sat inside and chatted.

A month later the woman looked like a new person. "I remembered what it was to be alive," she told Lustbader. The ailing husband, in a position with virtually nothing to offer, also benefited from this rare chance to give a gift to the woman he loved.

Stories like these make Lustbader's "Prescription for Caregivers" video compelling. Its candor, common sense and ideas make it valuable to caregivers as well as their relatives or friends. A caregiver can order the video for private use for $30 by calling (206) 462-5722. The price for agencies or companies is $85.

"Take care of yourself so you can take care of the person who is ill" is her theme. She recommends the concept of the Sabbath—one day of the week that's different from the rest. She asks caregivers to write five things they would love to do on that day that don't cost money. "I'd love to take a long, hot bath; just soak," one stated. "I'd go the attic and read some trashy novel," another declared. "I'd like to make a phone call without him listening in on the extension," a woman noted.

Lustbader strongly recommends that caregivers join a support group. They'll learn there that guilt is part of practically every caregiver's burden. It ranges from entrusting the care of a loved one to a stranger to the unspoken feelings of hostility toward family members who won't help. Also, resentment crops up. "Resentment is poison," Lustbader said. "It can be a line that cuts across your stomach. When that happens, you know you're doing too much."

The antidote often consists of the courage of telling the ill person the truth. In a support group, a caregiver learns that almost anyone can reach a breaking point, as in the case of the well-dressed matron who arose in one session and declared, "I hit my husband." And a real life saver is a sense of humor.

When Lustbader's grandfather was in the late stages of Alzheimer's, he stopped shaving and bathing, and refused his wife's offers of help. So a visiting aide was hired. When the attractive young woman arrived, he smiled and a gleam appeared in his eye as the pair headed into the bathroom. Later, he could be heard singing. When he emerged, he was clean-shaven and fairly glowing, much to his wife's discomfiture. "She never could find out what went on in there," Lustbader recalled.

Caregivers should watch for these red flags that are signs of nursing home placement for an ill person:

- No sleep for the caregiver.
- The ill person is too heavy for lifting.
- An Alzheimer's patient is approaching the end.
- Other outside stresses, such as the care of children.

Lustbader finds that the nursing home is not the main fear of those who are ailing. It is the fear of abandonment. When the move occurs, it often improves relationships between caregivers and their loved ones because visits to the nursing home focus on talk that means something. At home, the toll of nursing, cleaning and household operation short-circuits dialogue that counts.

I showed her video to a group of friends. They gave it a four-star review. Joan summed it up best: "I wish I'd seen this 15 years ago when I was caring for my mother."

Lustbader is the author of *Counting on Kindness: The Dilemmas of Dependency,* published by The Free Press ($18.95). She is the coauthor with Nancy Hooyman of *Taking Care of Aging Family Members* ($22.95) by the same publisher.

Some points to ponder

Here's a phone number worth saving: It's 1-800-677-1116. One reason is that real people answer when you call. But, more importantly, it's the number for Eldercare Locator.

It's a free public service you can call Monday through Friday from 6 a.m. to 8 p.m. when you or a friend need information about public agencies or private organizations that serve the elderly.

Here are some services you can explore:

- Meal delivery, transportation assistance and chore services provided by local home and community-based groups.
- Housing options
- Nearby senior centers
- Adult day care; respite from daily caregiving responsibilities.
- Financial, legal help and elder abuse prevention programs.
- Specialized services for older people with Alzheimer's disease, cancer, diabetes, heart problems and other illness.

You simply provide the county, name of the city or zip code of the senior in need of assistance and a brief description of the need that exists. You don't have to live in the same area as the person who needs help.

A trained specialist will provide information, including names, addresses and phone numbers, of resources and services available in the person's community.

Eldercare Locator is underwritten by the U.S. Administration on Aging and administered by the National Association of Area Agencies on Aging and the National Association of State Units on Aging.

*   *   *

Sixty percent of U.S. people 65 and up are women. By 2000, there will be about five women for every two men over 75.

Almost three-quarters of all elderly persons living below the poverty line are women, according to the U.S. Administration on Aging.

Women tend to lack income security because of their uncompensated roles as parents, grandparents and caregivers. When these activities interrupt their work patterns, they receive less in the way of health, pension and other benefits, the administration says.

Elderly women are nearly twice as likely as elderly men to be poor or near poor, according to a U.S. General Accounting Office report. People over 75 are twice as likely to be in the same fix compared with those between the ages of 65 and 74. Minorities also lack funds in far higher ratios than whites, the report said.

*   *   *

U.S. citizens over 65 will number more than 70 million in 2030. In 1990, their total was 31 million.

*   *   *

Ladies, see if you can recognize the man in your life in this description:

He puts off seeing the doctor even when feeling poorly.

He postpones treatment until his condition worsens.

He clams up when the topic is about health.

These are reasons why men live about seven years less than women, reports the Diabetes Advisor.

Men could regard themselves on a par with the car, the publication advises. They could learn about their personal factory parts and how they work. They can schedule regular maintenance and have things checked before rust develops. And they can talk about parts that aren't working they way they once did.

*   *   *

"Fern thought the ladies at bingo wouldn't notice the engagement ring George gave her last night."

"Did they?"

"Did they! Two of them recognized it at once."—*Aged to Perfection* (published by the Albuquerque (New Mexico) Office of Senior Affairs)

With all five children away from the nest, I find lots of room in the home except for the medicine chest.

What to do when your spouse dies

"Whatever you do, don't move to Arizona."

"And stay where you are at least two years. If you move any sooner, you'll regret it."

These were among the viewpoints of women in my perpetual sunbeam's aquatics exercise class. The topic: the death of a spouse.

The subject brings to mind the time an elderly colleague of psychiatrist Victor Frankl sought help for depression caused by the death of his wife. After listening patiently, Frankl asked, "What would have happened if not your wife, but you yourself had died first?"

"How terrible this would have been for her—how much she would have suffered," the man answered.

"Well," Frankl said, "this suffering has been spared her. But now, you have to pay for it—by surviving and mourning her."

The old man began seeing his own suffering in a new light. He could see a meaning in it, the meaning of a sacrifice he owed her. His mourning continued, but without the desperation, Frankl said.

So, after the 911 call, the ministrations of the para-medics or the police officer, the fog begins clearing a bit, and you try coming to terms with the grief and forego any rash moves. What next?

Call on friends, relatives, clergy, your mortuary, the senior center care manager for support as well as comfort. Many mortuaries provide help with obtaining copies of the death certificate and contacting the Veteran's Administration to obtain a headstone and flag.

Consider asking a daughter, a son or a friend to contact the newspaper about an obituary and inform distant relatives and friends.

Your clergy can assist with a memorial or other type of service and offer suggestions if pall bearers are needed and you want to invite someone to provide a eulogy.

Phone your lawyer and, if applicable, the executor or trustee of the estate as well as the union or veterans and other organizations.

117

If your spouse was receiving Social Security benefits, notify the agency of the death. Find out if you are eligible for benefits. Notify the insurance companies and any previous employers providing pension or retirement payments.

Here are some other contacts for your checklist:

Insurance agents for the car, house and property; banks or savings and loans; institutions with the spouse's IRA account; stock broker; accountant; financial planner; property manager; people who owe money and to whom money is owed; county recorder; post office; Department of Motor Vehicles.

If your spouse did not set up a trust, see a probate attorney before a month goes by. He or she will handle the affidavit and present it to the county recorder if the home and belongings are in joint tenancy. If they're shown as community property, the attorney can file the necessary petition to shift ownership to you.

The accountant can help file an estate tax return before the nine-month deadline. You may find it necessary to make changes in your will. Several central county senior centers provide will writing advice or you may prefer calling your attorney.

If charge accounts or credit cards are in both your names, you are liable for outstanding bills. Remove your spouse's name from the account if you plan to continue using it or else close it. Close all the accounts in your spouse's name only. Charges on these cards also are payable unless you're divorced.

Notify utility companies, department stores, clubs, cable TV and other businesses if a name change is necessary on their bills.

Women sometimes leave the telephone directory listing unchanged or forgo having it listed at all.

Having written the above and keeping in mind the adage, "The best way to get something done is to begin," I am now about to create a list telling where all my records are located, take a fresh look at my will, chat next Sunday with the pastor, and ask forgiveness from all the people I've talked with this past decade whose names I'd forgotten when we met again.

I'm still trying to follow James Thurber's advice. He said, "All men should strive to learn before they die what they are running from, and to, and why."

An overdue salute to service women

When asked about her military service recollections, Marian Fitchett says, "The farther away I get, the better it was."

Even at the time, however, the experience provided a host of pleasant memories. Following work for the Army Transport Service as a civilian, she served as a Marine in San Francisco's Depot of Supplies, handling liaison assignments and met her husband-to-be, William, in the city. He was in training as a bombardier. The wedding came right after he received his wings.

"I tell people I'm an All American girl. I worked for the Army, dated the Navy, married the Air Corps, and served in the Marines," says Fitchett, who lives in Martinez, California.

She became a staff sergeant by the end of her 1943-45 hitch and formed a number of friendships.

"We had sharp uniforms and were considered an elite group," she recalls. "There was no harrassment and we even went to the head of the lines."

All of which explains why Fitchett took time out to attend the October 18, 1997, dedication of the Women in Military Service for America Memorial in Arlington, Virginia.

Her hotel had booked 200 people but 600 showed up. "Four of us ended up in our room," she says. Estimates on the total attendance for the ceremony ranged from 30,000 to 80,000.

"It was impressive, a tremendous job, well done," she says of the three days of lunches, dinners, tours, socializing, and, of course, talks.

The memorial, located at the entrance of the Arlington National Cemetery, is a granite half-circle 226 feet in diameter and 30 feet high. Behind it are a theater, an exhibition hall and a registry for the the names and experiences of some of America's nearly two million service women.

(Former service women may register by calling 1-800-I SALUTE.)

A Hall of Honor pays tribute to those who died for their country and glass tablets feature appropriate quotations. Several observers noted that the tablets offer a reminder that some glass ceilings still exist.

President Reagan signed the bill in 1986 to honor military women. It provided some support and created a foundation that took on the job of raising all but $9.5 million of the total $21.5 million expense. As foundation head, retired Brigadier General Wilma L. Vaught was the driving force in creating the memorial.

Early in her 28-year career in Air Force, "Someone told me I couldn't do something because I was a woman." That spurred her to accomplish the task and continue striving, she said.

Justice Sandra Day O'Connor noted that 127 women, many of them disguised as men, are known to have served in the Civil War. It wasn't until 1948 that women were admitted to the services, but their numbers were limited to 2 percent of the men in active forces. The cap was removed in 1967 and women now make up 11 percent of the people on active duty.

Alice Engle, a resident of Rossmoor in Walnut Creek, attended the ceremonies and enjoyed meeting Freda Hardin, a 101-year-old World War I veteran who lives in Livermore. "The memorial reminds me of the Greek Theater in Berkeley," Engle says.

Her one-and-a-half year stint in the Marines pulled her away from her native New Jersey. "I never would have gotten to California otherwise. I loved it and didn't want to go back."

A good reason for that was meeting Joseph Engle in San Diego. The company he worked for was building B-24s, which were in demand just then. They married soon after the war ended.

"So the service changed my life," she says.

She belongs to the Women's Marines Association Chapter where good friendships evolved and she stays in touch with three of the "girls" from the San Diego days by cards and phone calls, especially since the death of her husband in 1994.

Phillips' Book of Great Thoughts and Funny Sayings *says, "I'm for women's rights. I think women should be equal to men—even though they lose some of their power."*

When children become a burden

At a meeting recently where she was giving the keynote talk to about 250 grandparents, Wendy Lustbader asked, "How many of you are caring for your grandchildren because your children are addicted to drugs or alcohol?"

About 200 raised their hands. Children of the other 50 were experiencing problems ranging from mental illness to jail time. So clearly this was not your normal type of gathering.

The offspring with problems sometimes move in, and start "borrowing" money from a parent who may need it for his or her own health care.

"It's hard to stop," says Lustbader, a Seattle social worker and author who gives workshops on this topic. "You're worried about them (the adult children) and feel that they've got you coming and going."

(People with this dilemma should arrange to see someone who can counsel them on the need to set limits and stop the abuse being inflicted on them, according to specialists in the field. Contact the Adult Protective Service or your area's elder abuse program. You can start by contacting the nearest Area Agency on Aging.)

The substance abuse problem has been growing with each succeeding generation, Lustbader notes.

If you spot a friend who looks like she's letting herself go—hair messy, untidy outfit, maybe a bit disoriented from skipping some medication—it could be be a case of financial elder abuse, she says.

> Substance abuse: a problem that's grown with each generation.

Your friend may have moved in with her children in order to protect her grandchildren. Or the addicted children have moved in with her.

When the older adults begin developing health problems and approach the point of needing assistance, family fights can erupt. One faction favors spending the parent's money on long-term care, perhaps because they don't want to be bothered, Lustbader says. The other branch of the family decides to preserve the inheritance and care for the older adult, a step that the parent may prefer because it may be the most loving solution.

In some cases, though, the brothers and sisters fight until it reaches a point where the parent's needs are lost. "I consider that emotional and financial abuse," she says.

Many families benefit from having a professional conduct a meeting in which differences can be ironed out. A considerable amount of planning must precede a get-together with the goal of discovering why certain family members avoid doing their share or resolving long-standing resentments, she says.

Lustbader asks participants to write wish lists that include problems and possible solutions. When these are passed around or read aloud, solutions may occur spontaneously. She then guides family members in reaching compromises. Finally, a signed written plan spells out the steps on which agreement has been reached so that a trial program becomes feasible.

Sometimes, to put the kindest possible term on it, there's an insecure son or daughter who believes the inheritance won't be fair, so he or she visits the parent's house and takes what's coveted.

And while we're talking despicable, there's the low-life who befriends an older adult in the mall or at the fast-food place, then, when a friendship blossoms, offers to work for the senior at a low rate. Next thing, the young person is using the senior's credit card, taking over the checking account and, finally, influencing a change in a will that disinherits the children, Lustbader says.

Wendy Lustbader has achieved distinction in the field of caregiving with her work, seminars, a video tape and two books, *Taking Care of Aging Family Members* and *Counting on Kindness*. Call 1-206-462-5722 for more information.

After reading about things some grown children and scam artists do, I can relate to the old curmudgeon, H.L. Mencken, who said, "It is a sin to believe evil of others, but it is seldom a mistake."

WHEN OLD SEEMS NEW

What makes you happy?

Your assignment today, should you care to undertake this mission, is to jot your prescription for a happy, fulfilling life. A brief sentence, a phrase, even a single word will suffice.

Adelé Larson developed this exercise recently and solicited comments from 58 adults from groups in her Marin County, California, home territory and a group of San Quentin inmates.

Two concepts tied for first place: spiritual power and good health. These categories each received 11 votes.

(As an added bonus for your participation, you will receive some illuminating thoughts by several of the world's great thinkers. For example, on the subject of spiritual power, St. Augustine said, "Faith is to believe what you do not yet see; the reward for this faith is to see what you believe." As for your physical condition, Emerson said, "The first wealth is health").

Larson's survey lumped love, understanding and acceptance together for the second place prescription. Ten people decided these were the key, even though Dostoevsky declared, "With love one can live even without happiness."

> Love, understanding and acceptance rate highly.

Nine participants believe the secret to happiness is peace of mind or the right attitude or mental power. In this arena, Dale Carnegie quoted Roman ruler and philosopher Marcus Aurelius, who concluded, "Our life is what our thoughts make it."

Tied for the fifth place prescription were healthy relationships and "Being able to do what I want." Of the first concept, St. Exupery said, "There is no hope of joy except in human relationships." Regarding the second idea, Elbert Hubbard believed, "Freedom is the supreme good—freedom from self-imposed limitation."

Helping others came next in this informal survey. Which brings to mind, "Generosity gives assistance, rather than advice." That's by a fellow named Vauvenargues, who isn't listed in the encyclopedia, but my perpetual sunbeam says it must be one of the pen names Ben Franklin used.

A happy, fulfilling life requires financial security, according to four of the 58 people surveyed. Four others said that success or achievement was necessary. And another foursome candidly wrote, "I don't know" what the prescription should say.

None of the San Quentin inmates, one-third of whom are lifers, equated happiness to release or escape. Many said relationships are crucial. "They feel that without close ties with wives and children, nothing else matters," said Larson, who often visits the prison as the counselor for a Toastmasters club she founded there. She's routinely advised when she enters, "If they take you hostage, we don't come in for you."

Part of her message in San Francisco Bay Area workshops she conducts focuses on change. "You want to participate in change, rather than being a victim of it," said Larson, whose trademarks include an assortment of unusual hats and an infectious enthusiasm. The ability to change comes in handy for the three stages of life, which are youth, middle age and "Gee, you look great."

Seniors also benefit when they hone their communication skills, especially the skill of listening, she said.

As a cub reporter, I asked an old-timer how to spot it when a politician lies. "It's easy," he said. "If he scratches his head or rubs his cheek, he's telling the truth. But if he opens his mouth and moves his lips. . .

Passing the treadmill test with kids

"Listen, I finally got my kid out of the house. I don't want to see any brats now or later."

This is a response senior and retirement center directors hear at times when they plan a program involving children. The fact that the grouch's kid is 48 years old, unemployed and a late sleeper may have something to do with the negative attitude.

But lots of seniors get kicks from mingling with, mentoring and motivating youngsters.

The Concord (California) Senior Center has a child care center across the street. On occasion the kids, ranging in age from 2 to 6, march over to entertain. Three times a year they storm the center and dine with the seniors. So far, the center hasn't succeeded in finding a food that saps the children's energy.

Seniors attending the lunch must first pass the treadmill test of director Diane Lorenzetti. Well, there really isn't a test, but there persists a suspicion that the older adults wearing hearing aids turn them down a notch. There's also an etiquette risk with kids, like the one who asked, "When are you going to die, Mr. Fuller?"

High school students pull their weight at the Concord center. They spend from three to six weeks helping in the office and at the travel desk or testing the pool room equipment. (Actually, they'd have to wrestle too many old-timers there to snag a cue.)

"The seniors were leery at first," says Lorenzetti, "but before long they were interacting with the students." The young visitors handle their assignments with cheerful enthusiasm, which proves infectious.

> The enthusiasm proves infectious

At the Martinez Senior Center, carefully screened high school students socialize one-on-one with incapacitated seniors. This gives caretakers a chance to take a break, go shopping or visit a friend, says Margo Spaulding, supervisor. You probably won't see the students' names on the newspaper's front page, but you can sleep easier knowing they represent a big majority of the young people in America.

Intermediate school students interview retirees residing at The Chateau retirement residence in Pleasant Hill. The reporters write biographical sketches of their subjects, then give copies to their teacher and to the seniors. It gives the journalists a look at life two or three generations back, and the elders see themselves from a fresh perspective. "It's a program that is very well received," says Lisa Regnier, activity director.

Concord Royale Retirement Living Center residents are blessed with a group of youngsters from the nearby Calvary Temple Church. "They visit with the seniors and entertain them occasionally," says Phyllis Womble, activity director.

By the way, this is not the church whose bulletin reported, "For those of you who have children and don't know it, we have a nursery downstairs."

As many as 200 teen-agers attend Friday dances at the Walnut Creek Civic Park Community Center. It's an activity unrelated to the Senior Club there, but one that makes taxpayers and parents happy. I mean, have you priced a new dance hall lately?

Also, kids entertain the seniors there regularly, and the seniors collect grocery store receipts for computers that go to the schools. And to keep the children purring, the center's Snappy Cats kazoo band plays at a nearby elementary school.

"Intergenerational" is the word used for these get-togethers. It rates right up there with "interface" and "continuum"on the woozy word hit list, but it's a major force now in America..

Illinois boasts one of the nation's best overall intergenerational efforts. Programs galore, conferences and summits, and ample resources characterize the joint endeavors of aging agencies, universities, businesses, and government departments

---

With help from my perpetual sunbeam, I intergenerated five kids.

Taking a chance for an "Afterglow"

Does romance ever blossom?

Renetta Voigt pauses an instant, chuckles, then says, "Not so you'd notice it." She's the co-chair and a member since 1993 of the Pleasant Hill Single Seniors Club, which meets at the senior center about 25 miles northeast of San Francisco. So she's in a position to know. Nearly 30 members showed for a preview potluck on the Sunday before St. Patrick's Day. Three of them were men.

Those who enjoy it played bingo at 1:15 p.m. Following a business meeting, the members picked up knives and forks at 3:30 for meatless main dishes, salads and desserts. And even those who fizzled at bingo could still afford the 50 cent tab.

Members take occasional gambling trips and dine out several times a year. All in all, the club promotes friendship and activities, but doesn't match what the mind's eye conceives from the term "singles club."

The scope broadens for the Singleship group at Lafayette-Orinda Presbyterian Church. More than 400 people born before 1945 take part, and marriages reduce the roster every now and then. It's possible people get hitched just to rest up. There's something going on nearly every night of the week and four times on Sunday.

"Twice a month we hold a TGIF get-together at the Embassy Suites or some other spot," says Edna Cunningham, who frequently appears in community theater productions when she's not on assignment as a nurse. "A monthly dinner attracts between 30 and 40 people, and as many as 20 meet for lunch."

The single seniors also take hikes with a walking group, play bridge twice a month, cut loose at a monthly games night, enroll in a music appreciation seminar at St. Mary's College, and about three times a year gather for a dance with the Shipmates, a group made up of people born from 1935 to 1955.

On Sunday, some of the Singleship crew attend an informal worship at 6 p.m. in the LOPC chapel, schmooze during the "Newcomers Welcome" at 7, check out what's coming up during the 7:30 announcements, then at 8 attend one of the four or five sessions presented by professional speakers on topics ranging from travel and relationships to self-publishing and "magnetizing" love.

Yes, this is an tiring regimen, but at 9 comes the "Afterglow" time when refreshments and socializing perks one up.

Counting the singles from all age groups, more than 4,000 participate in the church's program under the beaming gaze of Rev. Tom Schwartz, singles ministry minister. The program began in 1976 when Rev. Chuck Shields, then an associate minister, experienced the pangs of a divorce and realized he and others might benefit from a program that helped people talk, learn, exchange ideas and meet others.

Claudio Strazzabosco, a real estate broker and a public speaker, says, "Some women believe all they have to do is show up. They fail to see they have to bring something to the relationship." He's also candid with women who dwell on things going wrong in their lives. "This is not a pity party," he tells them.

The number of women exceed the men in all of the LOPC single groups, just as they do at senior centers throughout the land and at Rossmoor, the retirement community in Walnut Creek where 8,500 seniors reside. One bachelor who moved there was overhead saying, "This is like living in a candy store."

Rossmoor now counts more than 50 couples made up of people who met there. In fact, this qualifies them for membership in the Met and Married Club, which started in the 1970s. Members enjoy a two or three day trip in the fall, dine at a summer barbecue and hold a big dinner, appropriately enough, on Valentine's Day.

And Rossmoor has another nifty idea in "The Connection." This group of women meets to explore mutual interests and develop friendships.

Do you suppose cloning will eventually provide male parity so that widows can take another shot at matrimony, achieving, as Samuel Johnson said, the triumph of hope over experience?

Beauty and the beatitudes

The official title was the "Ms. Senior America of California Preliminary Pageant," but I call it cruel and unusual punishment. Consider the requirements:

First is the perpetual smile, although to the credit of the ten contestants in Walnut Creek they didn't always use the high beam.

Second, there's the talent phase. Put yourself in their shoes, standing up there in front of 450 seniors, nearly blinded by the stage lights, then having to sing or dance or say something.

Third, you undergo an interrogation by four judges. Sure, they call it an "interview," but, harking back to your working days, just what was it you dreaded most about applying for a job? Plus, the chances for a "bad cop, good cop" technique are doubled with a quartet.

Fourth, there's the matter of attire. Take a look in your closet and try selecting a couple of outfits for a theme called "The age of elegance."

Finally, you must declare your philosophy of life. Think of it. The best brains in the world during the last 6,000 years are trying, without much success, to articulate the meaning of life, and you get to sashay on this huge stage to the accompaniment of your tape-recorded philosophy. This goes on for four hours. Well, the 40 seconds probably seemed that long.

Credit is due those courageous contestants. Instead of turning on the sponsoring FHP Health Care representatives in revenge, they performed like troupers.

Added entertainment came from Tony Martin, who sang 11 songs in his first set and came back later with seven more and won a standing ovation, partly because he still provides a velvet tone and partly due to his offhand reference to being 80. He said some gushing women had greeted him in the lobby as "Mr. Bennett" and asked if he planned to sing "San Francisco."

Genial Jim Lange of radio and "Name That Tune" fame em-

ceed the event and remarked that just because there was snow on
the rooftop didn't mean there wasn't fire in the stove—a joke older
than the combined ages of all the contestants.

But at this point your attention is probably straying as you ponder the meaning of life. Here's what some of the women wrote:

The winner, Audrey Marshall of Santa Clara, says, "I believe
whatever we do we should thoroughly enjoy it. Life is too short to
do something that makes you weary, blue, tired or sad, so you
should never enter a pageant like this." Actually, I made up that last
phrase.

First runner-up Dee Lee of Walnut Creek believes, "If you're
not part of the solution, you're part of the problem." She follows
through on that by volunteer work for a hospice and Goodwill In-
dustries.

Second runner-up Lida Henne of Lafayette says, "I try to
achieve an equal balance in my life of work, play, love, spirituality,
learning and laughter." She admits to "building fires under people
by encouraging them to live up to their fullest potential. . ." This is
known as talent scorching, a corollary to talent searching.

Third runner-up Candy Farrell of Fremont states, "I believe we
should take responsibility for our own actions, instead of on circumstances or other people. . .Persevere. . .Enjoy life. Put at least
one fun thing on your 'to do' list each day."

Fourth runner-up Patricia Driscoll of Walnut Creek summa-
rizes her philosophy with "Gratitude. I am grateful to God for His
goodness." His influence was noted during her talent segment. She
did a stand-up comedy routine cleaner than Tide and Whiz combined.

Before the show began, the front row had five men and four
women. By talent time the number of men had increased by 75 percent. Does that tell you something about outer beauty or was it
age-related myopia?

I admit to being both myopic and a front row voyeur.

Finally—the secrets of success

Looking back to your adolescence, what characteristics seemed important in achieving a satisfying life?

Bobette Brown didn't give it much thought then, but as the oldest child in the Brown family, she became little Miss Dependable. She also developed traits of trying new paths to familiar places in Oakland, California, and an openness to new experiences.

As it turned out in a study of her and 500 other fifth graders started in 1928, the traits of dependability and "intellectual investment" were two of the key predictors for a life of solid relationships, satisfying work and stability.

A third factor, self-esteem, was lacking, she recalls, until after her marriage to John Conlin and a variety of jobs. A resident of Pleasant Hill since 1958 with seven grandchildren, Bobette Conlin still participates in the University of California, Berkeley, study. So do her husband and their three children, Dave, Christy O'Connell and Karen Croft.

"It's been a lot of fun," she says. "Most of us in the study never felt depressed. We knew we had someone to fall back on." Interviews with the researchers lasted up to three hours and the children never fudged on their actions or feelings. "The interviewers knew all about our backgrounds and they knew our parents, so we figured we'd be found out if we didn't tell the truth," she adds.

The latest book on the group, *American Lives: Looking Back at the Children of the Great Depression* by John A. Clausen, gives detailed accounts of six study participants, plus shorter profiles of a host of others and a complete summary of the findings to date.

Bobette Conlin did not find herself described in the book, but recognized many who were, despite the use of fictitious names.

Clausen believes "adolescent planful competence" is the key that helps youngsters make wise, realistic choices later in life. The competence comes from parents or guardians who bestow ample love, provide authoritative views of appropriate behavior and motivate children to do their best. Out of this comes the confidence, intelligence and dependability that help individuals succeed. Other factors include physical attractiveness and a family's socio-economic status, the author says.

Like many of the study participants, young Bobette received a clear message that women's role was in the home raising children, that behavior was influenced by the question, "What will the neighbors think?" and that children should be seen and not heard. As one woman recalled, "I was programmed for marriage." Clausen notes these concepts have changed a bit.

After her three children were in school, Bobette Conlin worked for a couple of department stores, then became a nurse's aide for a convalescent hospital and, later, the Veteran's Hospital.

In a recent questionnaire, 188 of the original group responded, along with 126 of their spouses. They reported travel provided the greatest amount of satisfaction, that, indeed, the best things in life are free, and about two out of three of them noted some loss of energy. Their greatest concern: becoming a burden on others. Twenty percent of the women live alone now, vs. 11 percent of the men, and the most common physical complaint is arthritis. The questionnaire included 465 questions.

Over the years the study participants gathered in reunions on the UC campus, newsletters kept them informed of the findings and friendships developed.

"We felt special," Bobette Conlin says. "I remember one of the kids saying, 'Somebody really cares about us.' As for it being the depression, we never were told times were bad. We didn't get discouraged. All the kids had holes in their shoes."

When it comes to research, remember Yogi Berra's observation: "You've got to be very careful if you don't know where you're going, because you might not get there."

Lessons from the Great Depression

Some of you remember salvaging worn out sheets. "You cut one down the middle, sew what used to be the outer edges together, then hem the cut section," says Jane. "People didn't throw things out in the Depression."

The topic of seniors and frugality reminds her that unneeded cribs and baby clothes were given to the expectant mother down the street, who passed them along to someone else after the infant grew out of them. Thrift stores weren't necessary. "Everything was worn out," she says.

Flour sacks became dish towels or undergarments. People grew their own food and bartered any surpluses. "Out on the farm we never thought of buying pet food," she says.

Some of these traits influence us today. My friend, Frank Bentley, just discovered that, by cutting off the bottom of his toothpaste tube with a pair of scissors, he's stretched his toothpaste supply nearly three more weeks. He's the type who saves $17 or so by changing the oil in his car.

He doesn't flaunt it, but he's also the wizard who can save two-thirds of the cost of replenishing his computer printer's ink cartridge when it runs dry. It's something technical like drilling a tiny hole and pouring in the contents of a bottle.

When traveling, he finds homes with rooms to rent and cuts his lodging bills in half. I prefer making the bread line—free loading on relatives and friends.

Alice was visiting a friend once who, when she finished applying her lipstick, blotted her lips on a Kleenex, one that she'd used before for the same purpose—not once, but seven times. And there was room for two more imprints when she finished.

B.J.'s mother used to double her mileage with toothpicks by breaking them in half. I find this too extreme. Ditto for recycling dental floss.

Quite a few of us here in the West could save money if we

awakened to the fact that this is a high desert, Mediterranean climate inland from San Francisco, says Philomena.

"I grow cacti, succulents, oleanders and olive trees," she adds. "And I don't have any annuals in the garden. That's to save money, but it's also because I'm lazy." Her water bill for the past two months was about half those of her Alamo neighbors. She does maintain a small square of grass in back for the grandchildren.

If you spend a lot of time in, say, the family room, throttle down the furnace thermostat and stay warm in the winter with an electric heater. By shutting off the furnace pilot light in the summer you'll save about $12. Alice lowers her gas bill by drying her clothes outdoors when the weather permits.

I save by operating a business at home. This includes dues for the writers club, some business-related books, newspaper subscriptions, one-tenth of the utilities, and part of the car expense. It was legal to write off my travel costs to England a few years ago because an article about the adventure sold to several newspapers.

You can do likewise with your photography, cookie baking or sewing, but the IRS wants you in the black for at least three out of five years or else you must furnish convincing evidence you're striving for a profit, not pursuing a hobby. I do not try to save money by doing my own taxes.

Since 1969 Andy Baltzo has been riding his bike to and from the Mt. Diablo Peace Center, which he founded then in Walnut Creek, California. That's a round trip of nine miles, which saves on gasoline. The exercise probably helps a fellow who doesn't look or act like he was born in 1920.

"In my early teens, I heard a speaker who convinced me to nourish my body," Baltzo says. "So I grow my own food and eat mostly fruits, vegetables and nuts."

My parents raised four of us in a variety of small homes in Denver during the Twenties and Thirties. When people ask how they managed it, I explain, "They took in boarders."

For times when you need a word

Downsizing. That's what our younger friends and relatives cope with today. In some cases their companies right-size them. In others, they outsize them.

Paul Rowan voiced these examples in a talk I heard him give recently. As it happened, Rowan himself was "displaced" in his job, so he created Transitions Management Group/Outplacement International in Walnut Creek, California.

Now, when a firm announces a "reduction in force" or declares "You are now surplus," he offers his services, easing the readjustment to unemployment and helping in the search for another job.

Other favorites in this lachrymose lexicon include "restructuring, "reengineering" and "retrenchment."

In our day, people didn't get this verbal run-around. Well, management, with a vague promise of rehiring, announced "layoffs," occasionally. But when I got caught goofing off at the St. Louis shoe factory in my callow, U.S.-barnstorming days, the boss barely looked up as he said, "You're fired."

Those two words told me quite a lot about my performance, a bit more than "We're outplacing you."

Don't get me wrong. If a company's losses exceed profits and there's no other alternative, the boss could say, "We're really sorry, but, because of the terrible bind we're in, you're being fired."

In the field of aging, some people rely on jargon that tells me quite a lot about them. I heard some fancy words at meetings prior to the White House Conference on the Aging, a session, by the way, that, for the time and money invested, produced returns smaller than a dimple on a dust mite's bottom. It deserved downsizing.

Maybe the experience that comes with age helps us identify some of this B.S. ("A euphemism," said H. L. Mencken, "for bovine excrement.") Older adults I know, for example, no longer cloak death with words like "passed on" or "departed" or "crossed over." Not too many funeral homes or churches realize this, however, judging from the memorial services I've attended recently. Perhaps there's hope, though, because it's been a while since I've heard about someone "departing this vale of tears."

When it comes to lucid finales, Walter Cronkite described an interesting scenario: "When I go, I'd like to go like Errol Flynn—on the deck of my 70-foot yacht with a 16-year-old mistress." Betty Cronkite responded: "You're going to go on a 16-foot boat with your 70-year-old mistress

On days when you run into folks with unfathomable argot, try this phrase finder and see if they can guess what you're driving it. Pick a word at random from each column and use the phrase in a sentence that you express with conviction or outrage:

Certified	collocation	paradigms
Independent	strategy	continuum
Comprehensive	focal point	parameters
Shared	system	agendas
Community	long-term	consortium
In-depth	sensitivity	cohorts
Pro-active	partnership	services
Staffing	multi-purpose	components
Institutional	societal	empowerment
Developing	quality	networks
Aging	assessment	infrastructures

Employ a few phrases from this batch and you'll impress, confound or alienate your audience. Maybe all three.

People in government, the Pentagon and lots of corporations cannot function without euphemisms. They could never call a spade anything other than "a digging implement." Euphemisms are their first line of defense against an irate bunch of voters, tax payers or customers. If you listen to them, they'll have you believing (in a nifty turn of phrase by Marsha Corrales) that a millennium is something like a centennial—only it has more legs.

Most of us know from experience the truth of Adlai Stevenson's comment: "Man does not live by words alone, despite the fact that sometimes he has to eat them."

Getting fazed by wretched excess

Last week's rerun of "Frasier," one of my favorite sitcoms, ended up with several scenes in a retirement home. The plot, in case you missed the show, finds his producer, Roz, picking up a disgusting assortment of trash with a road crew, performing community service because of a speeding ticket. She's chosen this untidy job instead of helping in a retirement home because she possesses a fear of aging.

Frasier persuades her that assisting older folks isn't all that terrible, and volunteering will help her cope with the fear. But after two residents die during her visits with them, others call her "The angel of death," and she reneges on the assignment. So Frasier escorts her back. Roz visits a woman in her eighties whose irrepressible spirit puts the prospect of aging into a far more acceptable, if not wildly anticipated, frame of reference.

I can just see, when the show originated, this team of comedy writers at work. Someone piped up: "Let's make this biddy a real rebel. Let's have her smoking a cigarette."

Sure enough, the scene finds both women puffing away—the senior in bed and Roz seated beside her. Neither of the women inhale and the manner in which they handle their cigarettes reveals they are amateurs at the pause-and-puff routine.

So instead of an unsullied, revealing relationship, the scene reeks with this phony byplay. Oh, yes. There's also the soaring cases of apoplexy across the U.S. among administrators of retirement and nursing homes where smoking indoors is verboten.

Meanwhile, as the ladies puff away, an alternating scene with Frasier and another resident, Norman, played by James Earl Jones—that fellow with the deep, mellifluous voice—achieves a humorous resolution tinged with poignancy. The action shows how the lead character, Kelsey Grammer, benefits from his study of Jack Benny's techniques.

I see few movies, but I'll generalize anyway because of the excess of action over narrative. Directors believe, "If that crash and explosion grabs 'em, we'll enhance the scene by making it twice as big and three times as long." Maybe it works the first time, but by the seventh catastrophe I'm worn out.

Even movie previews go too far. They reveal virtually the whole story.

These entertainment insights arrived shortly after the match between Holyfield and Tyson, a fight that sums up how closely boxing now follows on the heels of professional wrestling, which achieved wretched excess status 40 years ago.

A review of some newspaper headlines suggests the impact of a man biting the ear of his opponent:

"Ear-Responsible," Fort Worth Star-Telegram; "Tyson's Behavior Hard to Swallow," Providence Journal-Bulletin; and "Requiem for a Chompion," Philadelphia Daily News.

The reactions vary somewhat from the days of Joe Louis, a boxer who possessed an unassuming dignity, based on news reports, radio broadcasts and newsreel footage that I recall.

As long as we're on the subject of excess, there's the matter of contributions to politicians. Maybe we should pool all donations and let the recognized parties split the pot. We could also require the media to provide a fair amount of free coverage for debates instead of sound bites. We'd need to remember, though, what Groucho Marx said: "America is the only country where you can go on the air and kid politicians, and where politicians go on the air and kid the people."

Superfluity abounds today. America sports a surplus of men wearing earrings and women with tattoos. TV carries too many commercials and grocery stores display an astounding number of cereals. The county bus system opted for the biggest bus size available, but it's been more than two years since I've seen one at least two-thirds full. Gambling is lining the pockets of politicians with countless dollars.

I could go on but it would seem, well, excessive.

Like Mae West, I believe that sometimes too much of a good thing is splendid. In my case that would be sleeping.

Why not expect a miracle

Once again I am surrounded by beauty. Nonetheless, I keep my eyes closed, then I hear Mary say, "Welcome to the world." Next, Norma softly declares, "I'm so glad you were born." Elizabeth allows as how, "You are perfect just the way you are."

I am seated in the middle of a dozen women who agreed to employ the power of affirmations on me during a workshop.

Do real men seek cliches, I wondered when our leader, Karen St. Julien, coaxed me into the circle. By the time these 12 women finish massaging my ego with their upbeat sayings, my chair levitates two-and-a-half feet off the floor. Oh, sure, they're reading from a script, but they sound like they mean every word of it.

So, "Expect a Miracle," the title of St. Julien's workshop, works for me. But affirmations are just part of the resources we can use to feel better about ourselves. We're actually supposed to love ourselves.There. I've said it.

She says it's OK to do that. It isn't egotistical. It isn't sinful. But it sure isn't what my parents or grade school teachers would have suggested.

Self-love was not her strong point when she was admitted to a Texas mental institution. "It made the old movie 'Snake Pit' look like child's play," she recalls. Her depressed state shielded her from the worst elements of a six-month nightmare. The self-love began, appropriately enough, on Thanksgiving Day in 1984 when she found herself wandering into the kitchen and inexplicably saying, "Thank you, Lord, for me."

The turning point or, as she prefers, the miracle, helped see her through a divorce, two instances of melanoma, and the acceptance of an inner child who felt abandoned and unloved. Today she's under way on a professional speaking career to tell her story.

Dr. Bernie Siegal, one of her heroes, says the eight out of ten people who see him for treatment arrive in the world unwanted or were treated indifferently. Which helps explain why Bradshaw and others who talk about recovery from dysfunctional family life find big audiences.

The path isn't easy, St. Julien admits, and her higher regard for herself isn't constant. It's strong enough, however, to supply physical benefits. "If the mind can cause illness it can also heal," she says, quoting Dr. Siegal. She hasn't suffered a cold in four years.

"When I started having hot flashes, I said to myself, 'I don't care much for this,' and told them to go away." They didn't disappear completely, she adds, but they're down to intervals of only two or three minutes. Now, instead of hot flashes, they're tropic times.

She describes a lawyer who was told he had six months to live. He decided he would resume an interest in music during the time he had left. He joined an orchestra and was still playing years later. So hang on to hope, even when things look bleak, says St. Julien, a Concord, California, resident.

"This may sound simplistic, but I believe the lack of self-love is behind every problem that exists," she says. If self-love pervaded the world, individuals and nations would undergo radical transformations, she maintains.

"Yes, I still get depressed," she says. "But now depression is my friend. When it happens it tells me I'm avoiding something that needs healing." After her divorce, "being along was just awful. Now I relish being alone. I enjoy my own company."

She reads an affirmation aloud before retiring, then reads it again first thing in the morning. She also insists that you not put yourself down with "I'm such a klutz" or "I'm an old broad" type of comments. The subconscious takes it all in as though it's the absolute truth. So pat yourself on the back, treat yourself with respect, and try loving yourself. The life you savor could be your own.

Put this affirmation on your bathroom mirror: "I'm going to enjoy reading something from Senior Scene *every day."*

KEEP UP WITH THE TIMES

A "tempest in a tea pot"

"Can't you give me a pill and let me end it?"

The questioner, a 76-year-old man whose wife had died eight years earlier, was now battling the demons of alcohol and prostate cancer.

"So I asked him, 'Do you own a gun?'" said Dr. Forrest Beaty.

"I used to, but I gave it away. I was afraid after my wife died I might do something drastic."

"Wait a minute," the doctor replied. "You had the means to do it yourself, but you gave the gun away. Now you want me to give you a pill. It seems we have a contradiction."

Dr. Beaty mentioned this exchange in answering a workshop question about his profession's views on assisted suicide.

The American Medical Association opposes it, but, generally speaking, physicians assist the terminally ill patient with a more comfortable death, he said. Dr. Kevorkian's well publicized assistance in Michigan has made the issue a "tempest in a teapot," said Dr. Beaty, a man who quickly won the audience's respect when introduced as a doctor who makes house calls.

He emphasized that he was not advocating suicide and with equal emphasis advised seniors to fill out durable powers of attorney that spell it out if they do not want heroic measures taken in the final stages. Copies should go to the doctor, the executor, the attorney and anyone else who might be calling the shots when you can't. "Get it in writing while you're still in a sound mind," he added, which, in an election year, is asking a lot.

Thanks to some recent legislation, doctors are under a civil obligation to respect your wishes. But, without the durable power of attorney, it's possible the docs and hospital folks will be obligated to do too much for you.

Dr. Beaty noted that physicians sometimes get carried away with their own jargon. They like being in charge. In an emergency room study, doctors tuned in for the comments and complaints of patients for about 20 seconds, then the doctors took control. This suggests, said Dr. Beaty, that you take steps to ensure that your doctor listens when you visit. "Make a list and separate the objective points from the subjective, or emotional, points," he said.

Develop your own organized agenda, listing what's important to you. Include a rundown of your prescriptions, mention that you smoke or drink or have unusual dreams about Carmen Miranda. Well, save the dreams for your therapist. In addition to describing your chest pains, tell the doctor if your brother just died, because that just may influence what you're feeling.

His tips could be crucial if you're an HMO member, because some of them now allot about ten minutes per visit. HMOs differ widely, he added, citing a Newsweek feature that rated them. "It's an industry in tremendous turmoil," he said.

Tell your doctor in advance what you want to know about her or his prognosis. In other words, if you have six months to go, do you want to know? And if the outlook is bleak, remember it's just one person's opinion. An illness may run its course in a predictable amount of time, "but a vast number are unpredictable," said Dr. Beaty, who operates Physician House Call Services in Northern California.

"Doctors should have a game plan," he said. That includes prescription management and social issues that may affect you. And to spend quality time with your doc: "Try to get the doctor's last appointment for the day." The pressure's off, the end's in sight and chances are you'll get more than ten minutes.

"It's what you learn after you know it all that counts."
                                        —John Wooden

Yes, you can fictionalize your life

Writing about myself never held much appeal. The really good stuff couldn't be included for fear of embarrassing relatives or incurring a law suit. As for the rest, ho-hum.

But Elaine Starkman offers a tantalizing twist. "Writing Autobiographical Fiction" is the name of a five-week course she teaches at Diablo Valley College in an Emeritus College program.

"You can use some fiction techniques for those experiences you may not want to re-live," says Starling, who used the approach for her own book, *Learning to Sit in the Silence—A Journal of Caretaking.*

Which suggests I could erase the humiliation of the time Lois Johnson, my seventh-grade sweetheart, dumped me.

So just what is an Emeritus College? you might be wondering. When instructors and professors decide they've had their fill, they do not retire—they emerit. This means, when one is introduced at, say, a cocktail party, the introducer says, "This is Ronald Divocko, professor emeritus" whereas, in introducing you, he or she says, "This is Shirley Mishogo, who used to be in sales, or was it expediting?"

But, getting back to fictionalizing history, Fran Wojnar imagined what life was like for an ancestor, Eliza Korte, who was sent from Germany to America at the age of 16 with a younger brother to find a place for the family. Wojnar conceived letters that Eliza might have written to convey the trials and triumphs of the sojourners, who began their adventure in 1836.

Wojnar, a Pleasant Hill, California, resident, benefited from suggestions of her classmates in a DVC class, then self-published *Eliza, an Iowa Pioneer* in 1991. Thanks to a grateful Iowa audience, the book has gone into a second printing.

Another reason for writing: It's therapeutic.

Inga Ferris thinks so, at any rate. Her trip down memory lane helped her more than visits to a psychiatrist.

"I started with a creative writing course after my husband died," she said. The assignments brought recollections of her service in the Marine Corps during World War II. Scenes and the voices of her friends kept recurring.

She created a book about those days and even though she hasn't found a publisher yet, "I've been paid in the fun of writing it," Ferris said. And there's another bonus, especially with writing family history: The grandchildren will love it.

"Try writing about your feelings," she suggested for memoirs. Let your family know you're human and made some mistakes. As for things that jog the memory, dust off the old photo albums. Play some of the tunes from the 1930s and '40s. Listen to the radio stations that broadcast the old shows. Finish sentences like, "On the first day of school. . ." "Mama always told that. . ." or "I thought mom and dad would be angry when. . ."

She keeps notepads by the bed and elsewhere in the house and captures ideas, phrases, even dreams. If you're writing about a lecherous uncle, Ferris recommended a gentle touch. Say, "He had an eye for the ladies," instead of "Uncle John was a lecher."

Another tip: "Write it the way they talked." Dialogue helps bring people to life. Forget about spelling and punctuation, she insisted. Instead, focus on capturing the colors and aromas of the moment, the actions and reactions of people. As added spice, throw in some of the headlines of national or local news from the time you're writing about.

One of her sons helped the cause by giving her a box of eight audiotapes called "Home Front." They include newscasts, music and commentary about World War II days.

A splendid resource is the "LifeStory" newsletter by Letter Rock Publications, 3591 Letter Rock Road, Manhattan, KS 66502. The editor, Charley Kempthorne, put his tips from back issues into a book called *For All Time: A Complete Guide to Writing Your Family History* ($15.95 plus $3 shipping and handling. One of his recommendations is to join or start a family history writing group.

Stephen Leacock's view seems apropos: "Writing is no trouble: You just jot down ideas as they occur to you. The jotting is simplicity itself—it is the occurring which is difficult."

Focus a moment for fresh ideas

If for some reason you want to slice the apple exactly in half, start the cut from the bottom. The number of times your knife will split the stem will amaze you.

This tidbit results, not from watching the inescapable Martha Stewart, but from an experimental approach inspired by *Serious Creativity,* a book by Edward De Bono. He advocates an easy technique—which is exactly what I need in this area—he calls "simple focus." You might, for example, note the hot dog you're fixing for a grandchild. Would it be more fun shaped like a donut or in a circular patty? Maybe it could have vitamins inserted. Someone once thought of putting a hot dog on a stick.

De Bono suggests we spend a couple of moments a day focusing on items like hot dogs or on waiting in line at the store or the hole you dig for the bulbs, even if no attempt is made to develop any ideas from the item or process.

Case in point: After years of haphazardly filling ice trays, I now end up with uniformly even amounts of water in each little compartment. You just hold the tray at a 45-degree angle while the water flows. Excess amounts go into the compartment below the one where you started, and when the final section begins overflowing, you're done.

OK, this doesn't register a 5.2 on the Richter Scale of creative endeavor, but a person must commence somewhere. Recently I joined 13 other seniors on an experimental "Creativity Corps" project that convinced me seasoned brains still possess the ability to blossom with a fresh idea or two. And De Bono's techniques helped.

We gathered at the senior center with the goal of exploring eight topics and ended up with 131 ideas. It's true, some of them were, to put it kindly, off the wall. I mean, would you really want to hear a talk by the Abominable Snowman?

Well, it turns out that, yes, everyone would, but we couldn't produce the answer on where to find him. Often, however, from far-fetched ideas come practical ones. How about a senior center series on the world's greatest hoaxes ranging from the Piltdown Man to a Congress voting for election finance reform? The Corps members suggested workshop topics and activities such as "Living Frugal," "Sleep Therapy," a "Sadie Hawkins Dance," "Dream Analysis," plus a "Toy and Tool Swap."

The center supervisor, Nancy Whaley, got a charge out of this plethora of ideas, including one for seniors and school kids doing a role-reversal activity, first at a school then at the center. In between visits the participants would exchange letters.

Other ideas ranged from using volunteers on a sort of Welcome Wagon program for newly arrived seniors to a tie-in with Diablo Valley College's free screenings of significant movies.

By actually trying half a dozen techniques for developing ideas, Creativity Corps members are better equipped for handling life's little vexations or the heavy-duty stuff. The group, incidentally, had some fun later by helping two other nonprofit groups with ideas for innovative programs and fund raising.

The basic steps in creative problem solving begin with preparation. You round up as many facts and ideas as possible, then let your imagination roam, trying to hush the critic who sits on your shoulder saying, "Ah, this will never work."

In the incubation stage, you let the data simmer; you "sleep on it." The unconscious mind, that storehouse of all that you know, continues working on the challenge. Daydreaming, a walk in a park, a long shower—these are the times that often lead to that moment when you shout, "I've got it!" This is called the illumination stage.

Finally comes what often proves the most difficult of all, putting the idea into action.

For more and better ideas, experts suggest: 1) Capture thoughts on notepads. 2) Change routines. 3) Explore more than one right answer. 4) Visualize and affirm goals 5) Set a deadline. 6) Reward yourself occasionally. 7) Make a choice to be creative.

Carl Ally said, "Either you let your life slip away by not doing the things you want to do, or you get up and do them"

Check these to jog your memory

In *Phillips' Book of Great Thoughts and Sayings* is this truism, "The true art of memory is the art of attention." I keep telling myself that, but only after I've been introduced to someone and promptly forget his or her name. But there is hope for the memory-challenged, says Edith Manley.

Try chunking, she suggests. And, no, that's not an Orient trip program. For a phone number such as 682-6440, it may prove easier to remember in chunks of 68 26 440. As reinforcement, perhaps 68 is part of your address and 26, your age when your sweetie finally proposed.

Concoct a story as a memory tool. "Let's say you're dropping off some clothes at the cleaners, picking up material at the church, visiting your friend, Myrtle, and stopping at the library," Manley says. Interconnect these elements in a story with an opening, conflict, suspense and a climax. When I tried this, Myrtle found me so preoccupied she called my perpetual sunbeam in alarm.

About that dry cleaning. Dump those clothes by the front door and you'll not forget them when you leave. I put a two-week deadline on transferring my pile.

You can take the first letters of various items and make up a word or acronym, thus aiding your recall. With the errands mentioned above, however, "CCML" may not prove too helpful unless you're a Roman numeral fan.

Some people call their own answering machines and leave themselves a message as a reminder, Manley reports. Another helpful technique: "Write it down." she says. A journal or a diary often comes in handy.

Would you like to remember names for more than three seconds? During the introduction, repeat the person's name, perhaps even comment on it. As I was saying the other night, "It's a pleasure meeting you, Mrs. Dalrymple." A moment later I added, "Dalrymple; is that Norwegian?" She said, "No. It's British."

You also could borrow memory coach Harry Lorayne's technique of association. If he'd been there he would have linked Mrs. Dalrymple to a doll with a big pimple on its nose.

There's a risk with this method, as I discovered when leaving the party. I loudly declared, "Good night, Mrs. Barbyblotch."

When the person's name won't surface, I go through the alphabet hoping for a connection. Invariably it's Wilson, Yeager or Zenker, and the party's long gone before the memory's triggered.

At a seniors' health fair, an HMO gave me a plastic organizer. I put pills and vitamins in sections marked for each day of the week. At first I kept forgetting where it was located. Now, unless company's coming, it's on the dining room table because—I never forget to eat.

If there's a meeting you must make in the afternoon, set your alarm clock or kitchen timer, remembering, of course, an allowance for travel time. On some days, I set the alarm to remind me to set the alarm.

A pocket or purse calendar proves helpful, if you think of taking it along. The challenge is remembering to keep the wall calendar at home in sync with the portable one.

As Edith Manley emphasizes in her memory workshops, "Drink eight to ten glasses of water each day. Your brain needs those nutrients." And when visiting, try to not forget where the bathrooms are located.

If you exercise your brain, the memory improves. You might try Scrabble, crossword puzzles and a course in macroglobulinemia. You could learn a foreign language such as IRS Form 6765 R&D. It's also been said that you will improve your memory when you lend someone money.

You also could socialize with smart people. Join the Mensa Society, which is an organization of people with extra high IQs, and enjoy some scintillating talk about the cost of belonging, the location for next year's convention, and the latest episode of "Frasier."

I think I dislike most the phone call when someone says, "The meeting's getting under way. Did you forget?"

Spoils of poetry aren't for me

It's difficult describing my feelings about my poem. It was accepted by The National Library of Poetry as a semi-finalist in its North American Open Poetry Contest. Not only is it in contention for a $1,000 grand prize, or one of the 100 prizes of $50, it also will be printed in an anthology, "Endless Skies of Blue," scheduled for April, 1998, publication.

The 8 1/2 x 11-inch book will include more than 3,000 poems on about 500 pages. Poems are limited to 20 lines or less, which explains how so many can be crammed into one book. And guess what? I have the option of ordering it for a pre-publication price of $49.95. Additional copies are $35 each. There's a money-back guarantee.

But you're anxious, I know, to see this poem. So here it is:

Like the Daisies

By Theo Fuller
The path that leads to our place
Is bordered by daisies bright.
They welcome strollers all the day,
And the fragrance appeals at night.

Would it not also appeal if on our face
There was a glow, a radiant light
That, like the daisies, welcomed all who
   come this way
And enjoyed the pleasant sight.

Resisting the urge to call it "Bilge," I submitted the poem in shaky, handwritten script and selected Theo instead of Ted for my nickname. "Theo, you should be genuinely proud of your poetic artistry," wrote Howard Ely, managing editor. "We feel you have a special talent."

Let's imagine that 2,500 of the poets whose works were accepted take advantage of that special $49.95 price. That comes to $124,875, plus another $17,500, based on the required $7 each for shipping and handling. As long as we're assuming, let's say 2,000 folks order another book at a cost of $35 each for a friend or relative, so add $70,000 more.

A printer I called estimates that 2,500 top-quality hardbound copies of "Endless Skies of Blue" would cost no more than $30,000. Postage for the books would amount to perhaps $6,000, and another $6,000 would go for prizes. So The National Library of Poetry will make $170,375 on this book, less the cost of the initial come-on mailing. And this will be just one of a dozen books on various themes the company is currently producing.

Oh, yes. For just $20 more, I can order a brief biography printed in a special section available to the public and media. If 1,000 sign up, there's another $20,000 for the publisher.

"You are under no obligation whatsoever to submit any entry fee, any subsidy payment, or to make any purchase of any kind," the letter states. So that keeps it legal, but it certainly doesn't make this publishing practice any less reprehensible.

I've returned the release form, so the poem will appear in print. Am I ordering the book? No. If you'll permit me to adapt a line from the work, "The fragrance doesn't appeal day or night."

A month after the poem's acceptance I learned that "'Like the Daisies' is one of those exceptional poems than can be superbly presented, not only in print, but also through the spoken word," reported Ely. For just $29.95 each, a cassette tape of this and ten other of "our very best poems" is available.

As I tried dealing with this unexpected honor, imagine my surprise in finding that my poem can be printed on fine vellum and mounted on a walnut-finished plaque under Lucite for an added $38. If I take advantage of these offers, including one extra copy of the book, I'll be out $152.90. Multiply this by 2,500 poets in each of a dozen books and the publisher gets a net profit of about $4 million. Who says poetry isn't lucrative?

I've written a few poems, but I'm proud to say none of them matches "Like a Daisy."

Avoiding long-term care problems

People who are loaded should look into buying long-term care insurance. That's the advice I've read. One guideline says if you have more than $50,000 in savings or, as a couple, $120,000, check it out.

The rest of us should. . .Well, we might look at our lifestyles and make changes that reduce the chances of needing nursing home care.

Here are some ideas that can definitely prevent it:

- Deliberately get caught cheating on the nursing home admission exam.
- Submit a tape recording of one's snoring.
- Opt for a Kevorkianoscopy.

What are the odds of residing in a nursing home?

Forty-two out of every 100 Americans at age 65 face the likelihood of spending some time in one, says John Milgate. Of the total who do, 26 will spend one year or more.

The average cost in my Northern California county is $42,000 a year, and 48 percent of the people in nursing homes pay the cost from private resources by selling their homes, personal possessions, stocks and other assets, says Milgate, a Pleasant Hill attorney. A typical U.S. resident is impoverished after 13 weeks in a nursing home.

Medicaid picks up the tab for about 60 percent of nursing home residents—those who are down to no more than a house, car, household goods, burial plot, and a few thousand dollars, according to Health Magazine.

Medicaid's estate planning practice, however, lets families transfer assets, including savings and property, to another family member. This must be done three years in advance. If you establish a trust, it must precede your nursing home stay by five years.

The reason for doing so is to protect your adult children's inheritance.

California is lenient in the exemptions seniors can take in qualifying for Medi-Cal. If your spouse must reside in a nursing home, you may retain assets such as your principal residence, plus the boat and RV; household furniture and furnishings; one car; your 401k or IRA retirement funds as well as those of your spouse; certain annuities, term life insurance; life insurance with a face amount below $1,500; the burial plot; and the prepaid burial plan.

Thus even middle class and some upper middle class couples and single people can benefit from exemptions once designed only for the poor. Among Milgate's clients, the dollar amount exempted has reached as high as $410,000.

The best time to buy long term care insurance is when you're too young and healthy to need it. At age 55, you could have paid perhaps $430 a year for a low-end policy that covers $70 a day for nursing home care. The same policy for someone 75 years old would be about $2,100 a year. A really good policy would cost three times as much.

On the plus side, some insurance companies offer policies tailored to your needs ranging from nursing home, home assistance and boarding care. "You can pay for the care you want," Milgate told a Mt. Diablo Medical Center session audience recently. Some companies provide riders on life insurance policies. With these, the cost of care will consume the life insurance benefits.

If you've put off drawing up a durable power of attorney, you're going to cause problems for your heirs. If you have one and become physically or mentally disabled, you'll avoid guardianship since you've delegated financial responsibilities to the adult child or friend of your choice.

Milgate also recommends a durable power of attorney for health care. This gives someone you trust the right to make medical decisions for you if you cannot do so for yourself.

Distribute copies of the documents to the doctor, attorney, your executor and, if necessary, to the hospital or nursing home.

I admire the dedicated staff members and conditions of nursing homes I've visited. But reside in one? Borrowing a line from W. C. Fields' suggested epitaph, "I'd rather be in Philadelphia."

Forum explores strengths, needs

Independence. That's what seniors desire.

That's the reading I got from a forum conducted by the Martinez Senior Center. Independence wasn't listed as a pressing need, but it infiltrated concerns about transportation, finding help for chores around the house and safety.

"Senior Voices Speak Out" attracted 80 participants, about 70 of them women, willing to sound off. Well, we were also motivated by a free lunch, plus refreshments. I sat at a table with seven women, including facilitator Carol Hance, who, as a dietician, helps the county home-delivered meals program. She first asked our little group for thoughts on what's right with this Northern California city.

Friendly people, a fine climate and a big variety of antique stores and restaurants were some of the strengths mentioned. Martinez offers ample housing for older adults. Its senior center, under Supervisor Margo Spaulding, rates as top notch, my companions and virtually all of the other participants agreed. "I came as a stranger many years ago and got acquainted here quickly," said Ruby Weaver, who was preparing to celebrate her ninetieth birthday in a few more days.

No spot is perfect, and our county seat is no exception. In addition to the needs mentioned above, local residents believe frail seniors would like better care in the home. A surplus of potholes exists, and readers, bless their hearts, find the library closed too often.

I glanced around the table at my female lunch mates and innocently inquired if there was a need for men.

"Haw." "Pish, tosh." "Malarkey."

These were the kinder rejoinders. The response lends credence to my theory that a spirit of independence prevails, at least in Martinez. Either that or the men there forgo Miss Manners and deodorants, or pick their teeth in public.

Later, though, Claudia Whitnah, a retired teacher, had second

153

thoughts. "I'd get married again for rain gutters," she declared.

Carol Hance asked us for ideas on projects that would solve the city's needs, particularly the problems affecting seniors. We came up with programs in which high school students would handle household chores for older folks, seniors unable to drive would enjoy coordinated transportation, and, for the frail elderly, an evacuation plan in case of a disaster.

The filled-out flip chart pages of our group, along with the outpouring from the other tables, were posted around the room in "Issues & Needs" and "Potential Projects" categories. Next we received ten blue and ten orange paste-on labels, so each of us could vote for items listed in the two categories.

That's where the transportation, assistance with chores in and around the house, and safety surfaced as major needs. The "Potential Projects" voting favored things like a senior center van, taxi service for seniors and travel vouchers. Volunteers could take seniors shopping, to the doctor's or on pleasure rides.

Forum folks recommended a method of distributing information directories to elders who do not visit the senior center. Another possibility: start an auto repair course for seniors.

A tally of the suggestions and the voting will enable Steering Committee members to select a project or two that will meet the main challenges.

Will it work? Based on a similar 1996 forum for teenagers, the answer is yes. The gung-ho youngsters identified a batch of projects that led to a popular Club 21 and an after-school program with the Boys & Girls Club. A general forum in 1995 dealt with community needs and identified the teenagers and seniors as focal points.

Volunteers from county agencies, Kaiser Permanente, the city and businesses helped in the planning and during the forum. Kaiser also lent a hand on the expenses.

"I was so pleased with the participation of the people who were there," Margo Spaulding said afterward. "They were all involved in the process."

There are 23 antique and collectible shops in Martinez. Whenever I visit one, the owner wants to put me on display.

Words to think and dream by

Seen a good bumper sticker lately? They're scarce these days; or maybe it's my bifocals. However, these just in on the Internet:

Cover me. I'm changing lanes

Sometimes I wake up grumpy; other times I let him sleep

The gene pool could use a little chlorine

When there's a will, I want to be in it

Warning: Dates in calendar are closer than they appear

Always remember you're unique, just like everyone else

Lottery: A tax on people who are bad at math

Consciousness: That annoying time between naps

Ever stop to think and forget to start again?

That last one brings back a quote of William James: "A great many people think they are thinking when they are merely rearranging their prejudices."

Along the same line, Douglas Adams said, "Human beings, who are almost unique in having the ability to learn from the experience of others, are also remarkable for their apparent disinclination to do so."

When I admitted my proclivity for jumping to conclusions, a physically fit reader responded: " I often begin my day skipping an important meeting. When I do go, I run off at the mouth. By jogging my memory, I recall throwing my hat in the ring and hopping on the bandwagon when running for a political office. At the end of the day, you'll find me winding down."

In hopes of cranking him and other readers up, here are more morsels for cogitating:

This is the 37th anniversary of the year Richard Harkness told a New York Times reporter: "What is a committee? A group of the unwilling, picked from the unfit, to do the unnecessary."

"Madness takes its toll. Please have exact change."—Anon.

Barbara Hause, a luminary in my Toastmasters club, entertained us recently with a word game. I didn't jot it down, but because you've been kind enough to come this far, I've tried one myself. It's best read aloud:

A hig bero of fenior solks is Wohn Jayne. He cortrayed powboys in potion mictures. With a himple seartfelt, "Mowdy, Ha'am," he het searts of fomen wluttering. Ten, moo, kelt a finship with the pirile verformer. A mavorite of fine, Lophia Soren, trovided phrills with her putstanding oerformances. I also wiked latching Hetty Button in the cilm "Fircus."

Try running that paragraph through your computer's Spellcheck.

Did you hear about the frog that said, "Time's fun when you're having flies?"

It's included in a book called *Adventures of a Verbivore* by Richard Lederer. ("Carnivores consume meat; piscivores eat fish; verbivores devour words," says the dust jacket blurb.)

He confesses that words constantly whirl in his punster's brain. For example, your geography lessons acquainted you with Norway, Israel, Pakistan, Uruguay, Jamaica, Germany and Haiti. Here's the twist he applies:

"Little Miss Muffet liked neither curds Norway. Your leather wallet is fake, but mine Israel. My backpack is dark brown, but your Pakistan. I'm a gal and Uruguay. I see your daughter is taking piano lessons. Jamaica do it? An antibody will kill a Germany time. I love coffee but I Haiti.

He maintains that punning is a rewording experience, although he knows too well the loneliness of the long distance punner. "A good pun is like a good steak—a rare medium well done," Lederer concludes.

Some punnery experiments fail. When introducing myself to members of the opposite sex, I sometimes pronounce my given name, Theodore, as TheAdorable.

The yin and yang of nursing homes

Betty Geschwind's distinctive voice and ready smile come to mind while I sit here by the electric heater reviewing newspaper clippings and magazine articles on nursing homes. I met her at the first awards luncheon held for nursing home aides in 1990.

This Lafayette Convalescent Hospital aide was given the top prize by a CARE Committee formed for the purpose of recognizing these front line nursing home employees in the county. My assignment was to take her picture and crank out some publicity about the event. So from that meeting and from later award ceremonies, I learned a bit about the concern and caring that motivate many employees of nursing homes. It certainly isn't the money.

Recognition for outstanding care has made a difference in nursing homes in a period of change ranging from the acquisition of homes by chains to rapidly increasing numbers of the older adult population

Pleasant recollections of Betty switched to an unsettling October 27, 1997 Time Magazine article by Mark Thompson. He says seniors in nursing homes "are at far greater risk of death from neglect than their loved ones imagine." He cites one study that indicates 7 percent of those deaths in California result from lack of food or water, untreated bedsores or other preventable ailments. The chief cause is understaffing, Thompson says. "The Federal Government doesn't dictate staffing levels and state efforts at regulating quality are meager," he adds. State inspections that reveal violations led to penalties or fines in only 2 percent of the cases.

Thompson also says that residents who are visited often by family and friends tend to receive the best treatment.

What about nursing homes in central county?

"They have definitely gotten better," says Lois McNight, executive director of the Ombudsman Program of Contra Costa County. Her volunteers visit the facilities regularly, check out complaints and serve as a link between distant relatives and the residents. "We like to think that part of the improvement results from our influence," she adds.

Despite an occasional horror story, McKnight rates the nursing homes in central county as "pretty good."

California offers another encouraging note. A bill authorized dental hygienists to treat nursing home residents without a dentist's supervision as of January 1, 1998. The measure made such good sense, the dentists didn't even oppose it.

It will enable Annalisa Lunsford to broaden the treatment she's been providing since 1993. "I started my Visiting Dental Hygiene Service then," she says with the lilt of a Swedish accent. "I'm one of 12 hygienists in the state who provide the service."

I visited with her while she attended an Oak Park Convalescent Hospital resident in Pleasant Hill. Earlier she had talked with his family about the treatment. Now, bedside, she checks his chart for his general health and medications and asks how he's been feeling.

"I haven't been brushing," he says in answer to her question. "It's too much trouble." And, no, he hasn't asked any nursing aides for help because he doesn't want to bother them.

With an economy of motion she puts on her mask and gloves, spreads her instruments and attacks the plaque with a good natured resolve.

Hoping to take both the resident's and my mind off her probing, I inquire about things older adults might do to improve their teeth. We should consider a bedtime fluoride rinse in addition to using a toothpaste with fluoride, she says. "Even those with dentures should see a dentist once a year because the gum tissue might develop problems."

I find that a nursing home resident possesses one thing the rest of us lack—control. Says Annalisa Lunsford: "They usually tell you how much they want done and that's it."

Maybe I'll try that next time my dentist is drilling a tunnel in my tooth.

My dentist says he periodically cheers up a regular client by canceling his or her appointment.

Senior center site of shocking love-in

The end of a lengthy love affair takes its toll.

Almost an entire box of Kleenex disappeared during a farewell party for Dolores Lendrum. And the box was reserved for her exclusive use. The teary response, along with plenty of laughter, followed expressions of affection that ranged from poetry and song to plaques and hugs by 150 or so Walnut Creek (California) Senior Center members.

The occasion was a farewell salute to a woman who became a recreation supervisor 20 years ago, not suspecting that her family would grow to the current total of 2,085 older adults. She's taken on a new city job that includes organizational development and marketing.

"How can this youngster deal with seniors?" This is what the late Mary Rogers thought when she met the 5'1" Lendrum in 1978, who, at the age of 29, resembled a junior high student. Those misgivings, which were shared by nearly all of the 200 or so members then, quickly gave way to respect and admiration and, yes, love.

It takes more than amour, however, to build a successful senior center. Lendrum persuaded older activists to serve on an advisory board. She reserved a retreat once a year for board members and volunteers, gave them recognition, then split them into groups for brainstorming, exploring improvements for the years ahead.

With help from excellent staff members, she arranged health screenings, medical insurance and financial counseling, even pedicures. Classes on bridge, photography and computers evolved.

A trip program arranges adventures all the way from Carmel to Spain. Tai-Chi, yoga and aerobics help keep seniors fit. The nutritional lunch provides time for socializing as well as refueling. Aspiring students can learn ballroom, line or Polynesian dances. Sessions on current events keep people attuned to the present and genealogy courses link seniors to their past..

When some of the fellows asked about playing softball,

Lendrum gave them support. She did the same when several deaf seniors informed her they were looking for a place to meet. Today, the center's Deaf Club boasts more than 100 members who enjoy a variety of activities and events. At the party, it was a group of Deaf Club members who stole the show with their re-enactment of that first visit, then the results that followed.

Bob Freeman also scored a hit with his spontaneous invitation to dance, but I turned him down. Actually he invited the guest of honor, and she accepted.

"Dolores" was the song played by the Snappy Cats, a group that reflects Lendrum's role at the center. Lots of people, me included, yearn for the skill of playing an instrument. How do you deal with that? You encourage a kazoo-and-washboard playing group that wears leopard-like vests and cat ears. This feline flock also entertains at nursing homes and retirement residences.

Gil Smith employed a ruse I plan on copying. "I'm here representing 123 members of our eight softball teams," he declared. "Each one of them asked me to give you one of these," Smith added as he began kissing Lendrum, but he stopped upon seeing a restive Rick Lendrum preparing to vacate his post behind a TV camera.

Dora Mae Ipsen, the center's poet laureate, saluted Lendrum for friendship, which is, "feeling completely natural with another / Forgetting all pretense. . . / To be there when needed with that understanding word of encouragement. . . / We'd like to be the sort of friend that you have been to us. . ."

Master of Ceremonies Eunice Allen, trying to act like drill sergeant, kept most of the audience under control despite the prurient nature of the meeting.

Even if it gives Walnut Creek a reputation, I must say that as farewell parties go it was a love fest. And from what I've seen of Dolores Lendrum's successor, Linda Ausplund, this same sort of shocking behavior will be continuing.

"Love, you know, seeks to make happy rather than to be happy," said Ralph Connor, and that seemed appropriate for the scandalous display I witnessed.

Smile a While

How Bible heroes lived sooo long

The intriguing subject of aging drew me to the Bible last week. I searched for clues about people like Methuselah, who lived 969 years, and Sarah, who gave birth to Isaac at the age of 90 and lived until the age of 127.

What factors helped them and many of their descendants rack up all those years? Also, how about the ability of some of Methuselah's offspring to sire children at 180 or better?

These were among the questions I put to Malcolm Barkley, a gerontologist and former pastor of the Church of Longduration.

"First," said Barkley, "you should recall that these were the days before Sir Walter Raleigh, sort of an advance man for Phillip Morris. No cigarettes, pipes or stogies affected these ancestors. Oh, some of the weaker tribe members were shoved to the downwind side of campfires and experienced lung damage and singes. There's also the element of 'What you don't know won't hurt you,' as this anonymous poem indicates:

'Methuselah ate what he found on his plate,
And never, as people do now,
Did he note the amount of the calorie count;
He ate it because it was chow.

'He wasn't disturbed as at dinner he sat,
Devouring a roast or a pie,

To think that it lacked in granular fat
Or was a few vitamins shy.

'He cheerfully chewed each species of food,
Unmindful of troubles or fears
Lest his health be hurt by a sweet dessert;
And he lived more than 900 years.'"

"That's an interesting point," I said. "How about things like the drinking water?"

"Residents in Canaan and Babylon enjoyed clear well water filled with nutrients, but low on salt," he said. "On the other hand, Sodom and Gomorrah. . .Well, the drinking there was spirited. God saw to it that they didn't set any longevity records."

"I noticed that Noah became the father of Shem, Ham and Japheth after the age of 500. How do you account for that?"

"Noah grew up in the Ararat Mountain region, a land of abundant plant life but not much in the way of small or big game. Consequently, people living there grew up as vegetarians—lean and mean and, ah, virile," Barkley said.

"But more than 500 and still. . ."

"You must understand," he continued, "some of the common foods then would be called aphrodisiacs today. It resulted from the, ah, virgin soil conditions."

"How can I obtain some," I asked. "The soil, that is."

"Unfortunately, with society's use of pesticides, autos and perfumed magazine pages, crop-growing conditions now can't match those of nearly 2,500 years ago," Barkley said.

"It says in the Bible that Sarah laughed when God announced she would conceive at the age of 90," I said.

"Yes. As I recall God chided her for that. But heaven knows why."

Noah got all the animals off the ark except a pair of snakes. "Go forth and multiply," he told them. "We can't," one replied sadly. "We're adders." Research revealed that it was Noah's son, Ham, who thought of this joke.

Why spats and cranks vanished

Everyone knows why rug beaters went the route of the butter churn: It was the operators who ended up beat.

But you may not know the reasons why other devices, products and practices disappeared or dwindled in popularity. Here, then, are the official explanations:

Pull-chains on commodes fell from favor when Phelan Flusher pulled a chain too hard one day and the wall-mounted reservoir cascaded on him. Fortunately for us, he felt so irked he invented the toilet tank that we rely on today. Poor Flusher, though, couldn't see that he'd also invented the bathroom shower, so he never capitalized on it.

Sen Sen provided a cover-up for people who forgot to brush their teeth or had been swigging beverages made in bathtubs. When conversing with others, a Sen Sen user overpowered them with an aroma like hot asphalt. After the repeal of prohibition, improvements in aerosal cans and Pepsodent's invention of halitosis, Sen Sen's popularity declined, although street crews still use it for patching potholes. Meanwhile, Pepsodent ended up where the yellow went.

Blackboards got a bum rap in America's schools after a rumor started that green boards muffled the sound of a fingernail scraping across the surface. It originated with the company that produces the green covering. Oil companies achieved the same type of switcheroo by bad-mouthing street cars and persuading cities to buy buses using gas.

The scythe evaporated from the country's farms after mechanization and a survey that showed only 3.7 percent of the populace could correctly pronounce the word. Fewer than half of them could spell it.

Spats proved popular in the days before women and men wore hosiery. The spats covered dirty ankles and provided warmth. When hosiery and daily ablutions became *de rigueur*, spats were relegated to closets as moth catchers. Men's socks initially lacked gripping power, so garters held them up. Thanks to elastic and Velcro, youngsters could then convert garters into ammunition for rubber guns, but Saturday night specials made those snappy weapons obsolete.

Kerosene lamps once illuminated the indoors, a development that relieved many whales because they disliked making oil donations for the whale lamps previously in vogue. Then the Thomas, Alva & Edison Company, after countless efforts to develop a coin-operated meter to measure it, invented electricity. The rest, as they say, is history that appears on your monthly light bill.

Ice cream sodas no longer rejuvenate at drugstore fountains, mainly because drugstores no longer boast soda fountains.

Rouge has faded in the changes for cosmetics. Bright red, and, for that matter, green, purple and orange, are the hair colors of choice for today's youth, whereas cheeks are ashen.

Except for senior center card games, few cranks exist today. They were necessary for the starting of Model T Fords. As an engine turned over, the erratic crank caused the operator to follow suit. If we still crank-started cars in today's litigious society, Ford would be mired in Chapter 11 proceedings and personal injury lawyers would need plastic surgery to erase their smiles.

Stereopticons gave us 3-D without glasses and the View Master proved a hit with kids. When advertisers discovered they couldn't air commercials on either medium, they bought all they could lay their hands on, except for the few now in museums and private collections. Today, TV furnishes the pictures, producing glazed expressions and curvature of the spine.

Corsets exerted a lot of compression in years gone by. This created swifter blood flow to the brains of wearers to the degree that they wisely discarded the garments, which Fiendricks of Hollywood redesigned for women with cerebral anemia.

It was Henry Ford who said, "History is more or less bunk,"and my account of how and why things happened reveals he had a talent for understatement.

It's not a chain, it's a link letter

Dear Reader:

Because chain letters offer unachievable expectations, please regard this as a link letter, which is not to be confused with the retired TV star, Art Linkedletter.

It was started by a citizen upset by Medicare fraud, problems with the health care system, and monetaphobia—a fear of having no money.

There is no expense for taking part in the links this letter offers and it is absolutely legal per Title 13, Section 1302 (b). Simply send one senior 65 years of age or older, in good to excellent health, to each of the five people whose names are shown below. (That's a total of five seniors; do not send just one senior to all five people.) Mail them first class, then remove the name in the letter's No. 1 spot and add your name and address at the bottom.

Within 14 to 20 weeks, when your name appears at the top of the list, you will receive approximately 16,740 seniors. If someone errs and sends you a sick senior, put a "Refused" stamp on his or her forehead and promptly return.

At this point you will form a company and establish a health maintenance organization, or HMO, and sign up the seniors. The federal government will then begin paying you approximately $400 per month per senior for their Medicare payments.

Of the $80,352,000 per year you receive for your seniors, you will spend about $20 million for their various ailments. For suggestions on what to do with the rest of the funds, contact *Senior Scene* and for a nominal 12 percent we will be pleased to provide you with ideas guaranteed to please you.

Do not break this link. A man in Topeka did so and he received 3,579 aluminum siding salespeople, 1,488 Amway distributors and William Buckley.

Send your seniors to these individuals:

1. Ava Rice, 978 Pinkham St.,Wartburg, TN 37887

2. I. G. Reedy, 1302 Flout Rd., Swink, CO 81077
3. Sal Fish, 830 Blinker Ave., Grubville, MO 63041
4. V. Oracious, 95 Higgeldy St., Germfask, MI 49836
5. Mercy Nary, 1494 12th Ave., Igo, CA 96047

Here are some case histories of people who have benefited from the link letter:

Malcolm Sharpe—"I was flat-as-a-bug-on-the-windshield-of-a-speeding-car broke when I received a copy of this letter. Usually I deep-six letters that sound too good to be true, but I have a soft spot in my heart for seniors. During the twelfth week my first seniors arrived and by the end of the 19th week, 15,326 showed up.

"Whereas I was experiencing problems supporting both the government and my family, I now am the owner of a new yacht, a new Lexus and a new condominium complex. My neighbors love me because I farmed out my seniors in the community; they did chores and baby sitting in exchange for their board and room until I incorporated."

Viola Turnbright—"I must have read and thrown away two dozen proposals like this, but this link letter clutched the tentacles of my heart, because it is my goal to leave this world a better place than the mess I found it. After my seniors began flowing in, I welcomed them with open arms. By the 15th week and the 14,389th senior, my arms were tired, let me tell you.

"We had such fun getting acquainted. The local food bank was a bit hard pressed at first, but things worked out well since nearly 100 percent of the seniors wanted to lose weight anyway."

Rufus Hollisteer—"The seniors started arriving after 15 weeks and at first it was a bit awkward, but my cousin, Jethroe, a tour guide at Alcatraz, worked out a satisfactory place for them. I've been offered $76 million for my HMO, but I'm in this for the big haul. I provide benefits such as wine country tours and attendance at Geraldo's talk show. Right now I have three tax lawyers looking at ways I can keep more of the $54.7 million net that's come in this year."

All went well with the HMO I formed last year until the drive-in, self-service operating room led to an uprising.

Relationship rules to live by

Remember Thoreau's observation: "Any fool can make a rule, and every fool will mind it." With that caveat, let us now explore. . .

Rules of Successful Senior Relationships

1. When you first meet someone, quickly repeat his or her name two or three times. Otherwise at our age the moniker or the person soon evaporates.

2. When you start chatting, forego the details of your infective endocarditis and ask others about something that interests them: the grandkids, for example, or the COLA increase or a nice nap.

3. As you explore mutual interests, limit the use of "I." An exception to this is when praising the other person, as in "I like the way those earrings shape your ears into giant exclamation points."

4. When you encounter a chatterbox, introduce him or her to someone similarly inclined, then reward yourself with a glass of punch.

5. Drop your facade and level with other people; be transparent. They, of course, will then be able to see right through you.

6. Some older people focus on their ills such as their regularity or, more often, their irregularity. Cope with the latter by giving them cards that the Prune Advisory Council will furnish you free.

7. If you goof with a comment about, say, her husband, who, unknown to you, has run off with a 40-year-old bimbo, take her mind off the subject by spreading *pate* on your shoe; insert in mouth.

8. If the other party asks for a date and you're already attached, bless them. Direct a male inquirer toward the senior center and a female to a philosophy or sailing class where they'll meet plenty of prospects.

9. When the person mumbles, step closer and respond in loud tones. Carry ear plugs for times when the situation is reversed.

10. If the person is an attorney, forego asking for advice about your personal affairs, especially if they know your address. The same applies to physicians and questions regarding your health. You never know what they're billing for these days.

11. If the person says, "I'll be perfectly frank with you," assume he or she will be hedging.

12. If you ask someone, "How are you?" you have only yourself to blame when he or she takes the next 15 minutes telling you.

13. When the person with whom you're chatting bores you out of your skull, tell them, "I totally disagree," then pause and ask, "What was it you said?"

14. Observe the law postulated by Leo Hanbury: "Small talk drives out meaningful talk."

15. If one person in a group insists on arguing with you, be grateful in the knowledge that at least one is listening.

16. While engaged in conversation remember the middle of the road is the best place to get run over.

17. Remember Wilson Mizner's advice: "Be nice to people on your way up because you'll meet 'em on the way down."

18. If you like short answers, wait until the other person has just taken a bite to ask the question.

19. If a bore brags about being a self-made man or woman, tell them, "That relieves the Almighty of a great responsibility," then credit Horace Greeley for the thought.

20. Accept others the way they are. If you can't, remember absence keeps the heart from foundering.

21. When you forget the other person's name, come right out with it. That is, admit your lapse by saying, "I rarely forget a name, but in your case it seems justified," to paraphrase Groucho Marx.

22. If the other party spills a beverage on you, put them at ease with a comment such as, "Well, it looks like the drinks are on me."

23. When you meet a know-it-all, ask for his or her opinion. You might as well, says Robert Orben, because you'll get it anyway.

24. If people raise their eyebrows when you return to the punch bowl, borrow Oscar Wilde's line. Say, "I couldn't help it. I can resist everything except temptation."

If you break one of these rules and people ostracize you, think how much better off you'll be.

Recipes for successful aging

Ruth Bernhard, a highly regarded photographer and a senior, offers this "Recipe for a long and happy life":

1. Never get used to anything.
2. Hold on to the child in you.
3. Keep your curiosity alive.
4. Trust your intuition.
5. Delight in simple things.
6. Say "yes" to life with passion.
7. Fall madly in love with the world.
8. Remember: Today is the day!

    *   *   *

A friend sends along these tips:

Discipline yourself to continue expanding and learning, keeping your mind active and open.

Enjoy the feeling that somebody else is in charge; you don't have to make decisions.

    *   *   *

According to Eric Tainter, "A person is not old until regrets take the place of dreams." He also said, "Happiness is that peculiar sensation you acquire when you're too busy to be miserable."

    *   *   *

From the Internet comes these thoughts about things people have learned as they aged: They said,

"I learned that even when I have pains, I don't have to be one. (Age 82)

"If you pursue happiness, it will elude you. But if you focus on your family, the needs of others, your work, meeting new people, and doing the best you can, happiness will find you. (Age 65)

"Life sometimes gives you a second chance. (Age 62)

"It pays to believe in miracles. And to tell the truth, I've seen several. (Age 73)

"You shouldn't go through life with a catcher's mitt on both hands. You need to be able to throw something back. (Age 64)

"Every day you should reach out and touch someone. People love that human touch—holding hands, a warm hug, or just a friendly pat on the back. (Age 85)

"Whenever I decide something with kindness, I usually make the right decision. (Age 66)

"I've learned that I still have a lot to learn." (Age 92)

*   *   *

While on their fishing boat, the husband, concerned about a possible emergency, said to his wife, "Please take the wheel, dear. Pretend I'm having a heart attack and you must get the boat safely to shore" She did so.

That evening, she walked into the living room where he sat watching the tube, switched the TV channel and said, "Please go into the kitchen, dear. Pretend I'm having a heart attack. You must set the table, cook the dinner, and wash the dishes."

*   *   *

Don't worry about avoiding temptation. As you grow older, it will avoid you.

The aging process could be slowed if it had to work its way through Congress.

Don't take life so seriously—it's not permanent.

*   *   *

Sign seen on a veterinarian's window:

Dog or cat spayed or neutered - $5

Senior - $2

From a senior center newsletter story about staff changes: "Please bare with us as we acclimate and move forward for a better future."

"When men reach their 60s and retire, they go to pieces. Women go right on cooking."—Gail Sheehy

T-shirt message: "At my age I've got an achy breaky every-thing."

Another T-shirt: "The older I get the better I was."

*   *   *

"It is time to be old, to take in sail."—Emerson

But, says E.B. Skinner, "It is not a time to be wholly adrift."

Burma Shave reprise

In my self-appointed role as a senior seer, it pleases me to predict a rebirth of interest in poetry here in America.

Hark back to your grade school days when teachers routinely required you to memorize the classic poems, an exercise that not only improved your brain's capabilities, it also bolstered your claim to cultural fame. Well, that's what Mrs. Murphy told her pupils.

But the major impetus for poetry appreciation, starting in 1925, came not from youth but the unlikely source first known as Burma-Vita, then, finally, Burma-Shave. At the start of the campaign, small signs on pine boards salvaged from barns carried conventional bromides, all in capital letters. Soon the messages appeared in catchy couplets proclaiming, for example, along one stretch of highway: "He played / a sax / had no B.O / but his whiskers scratched / so she let him go / Burma-Shave."

It was an era when suppliers of other grooming accessories shouted in print about your body's pungent aroma, crinkly skin and generally miserable appearance, according to *The Verse By the Side of the Road* by Frank Rowsome, Jr. Whimsical Burma-Shave signs provided a fetching counterpoint with the likes of: "The answer to / a maiden's / prayer / is not a chin / of stubby hair. . ."

Alexander Woollcott once said that it's as difficult to read one Burma-Shave sign as it is to eat just one salted peanut. The captivating ads proved addictive to entire families, truck drivers and, for a while, horses traveling the country's roadways.

(Horses loved to scratch their backs on signs on 9-foot poles. They broke so many, though, the company installed 10-footers.)

The ad campaign boosted sales to the point where one executive would later declare, "We never knew there was a depression."

It began with a liniment Clinton Odell developed in Minneapolis. He changed it into a brushless shaving cream, but American men weren't ready to forsake their strops and brushes even for concoctions from Burma. That mood prevailed until men and women began reading and reciting the likes of: "His face was smooth / and cool as ice / And oh Louise! / he smelled / so nice. . ."

Odell's son, Allan, who wrote most of the initial rhymes, could also skewer the competition, as in: "Beneath this stone / lies Elmer Gush / Tickled to death / by his / shaving brush. . ."

Electric razors also got their due: "A silky cheek / shaved smooth / and clean /is not obtained / with a mowing machine. . ."

My favorite goes like this: "Every shaver / now can snore / six more / minutes / than before. . ."

It seemed most of America's adults penned poetry after Burma Shave started a series of contests for the jingles. As many as 50,000 entries arrived for a single contest, vying for a $100 prize. Some were bad, some were bawdy, but the best succeeded like apple pan dowdy. One of the rejects said: "The other woman / in his life / said "Go back home / and scratch / your wife. . ."

The firm pioneered public service ads with "Keep well / to the right / of the oncoming car/ Get your close shaves / from the half-pound jar. . ." Police chiefs and highway patrol administrators swore the poems reduced car accidents and injuries.

As speed limits grew so did the sign size from 12 to 18 inches high and to 40 inches wide. The distance between each sign increased from 100 to 150 feet, so motorists could see: "She put / a bullet / thru his hat /but he's had / closer shaves than / that. . ."

When Philip Morris acquired Burma-Shave in 1963, the signs were soon phased out. There are still a few left today in the Smithsonian, including Allan Odell's favorite: "Within this vale / of toil / and sin / your head grows bald / but not your chin. . ."

By now you may be wondering, "What the dickens does all this have to do with a renaissance in poetry. Well here's a case / for greater / poetry / You can watch / B-S signs / on your TV.

Yes, the American Safety Razor Company, which now owns the rights, is investing $1.5 million in CNN and ESPN commercials between now and the end of the year to "return Burma-Shave to its proper place on the American face."

I'd still like to know why my face grows hair but the scalp won't.